Landscapes of
MENORCA

a countryside guide
Seventh edition

Rodney Ansell
revised by Sunflower Books

SUNFLOWER BOOKS

Seventh edition © 2023
Sunflower Books™
PO Box 36160
London SW7 3WS, UK
www.sunflowerbooks.co.uk

ISBN 978-1-85691-551-9

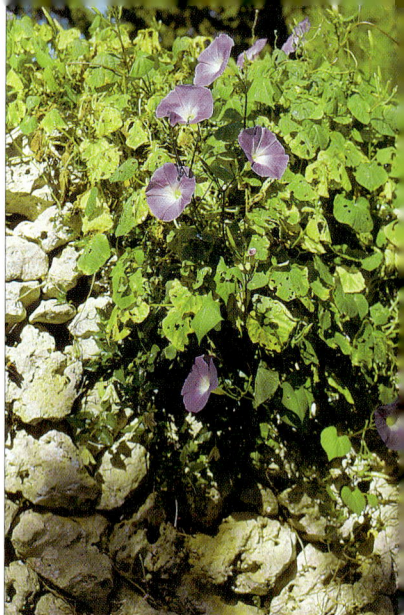

Important note to the reader

We have tried to ensure that the descriptions and maps in this book are error-free at press date. The book will be updated, where necessary, whenever future editions are printed. It will be very helpful for us to receive your comments (sent in care of the publishers, please) for the updating of future editions.

We also rely on those who use this book — especially walkers — to take along a good supply of common sense when they explore. While walls and gates enclosing private land cause the most problems for walkers on the island (see the article on page 42), *storm damage may make a route unsafe at any time*. If the route is not as we outline it here, and your way ahead is not secure, return to the point of departure. *Never attempt to complete a tour or walk under hazardous conditions!* Please read carefully the country code on page 10, the walking notes on pages 30 and 31, and the introductory comments at the beginning of each tour and walk (regarding road conditions, equipment, grade, distances and time, etc). Explore *safely*, while at the same time respecting the beauty of the countryside.

Cover photograph: lighthouse at Favàritx at sunset (Car tour 1)
Title page: Talatí de Dalt (Picnic 5; Car tour 2; Walks 7 and 8)

Photographs: pages 33, 39, 52-3, 96 (Hans Losse); pages 56, 56-7, 62, 76 (top), 76-7, 101, 102, 118, 123 (bottom), 115, 129 and cover (Shutterstock); pages 30, 31, 41, 82-3, 128, 129 (all), 131, 132: Sunflower Books; all other photographs: Rodney Ansell
Maps by the author and Sunflower Books, based on Spanish military maps (with kind permission of the Servicio Geográfico del Ejército)
Drawings by John Theasby
A CIP catalogue record for this book is available from the British Library.
Printed and bound in England: Short Run Press, Exeter

Contents

Ploughing with a donkey near Sant Lluís (Car tour 1, Walk 12)

SOME FEATURES OF THE MENORCAN LANDSCAPE

4

☀ Preface

Menorca is the island people fall in love with … the one they go back to year after year, the island where they go to retire. And no wonder. For in addition to all the normal attractions you expect from a holiday island — lively resorts, good safe beaches, day-long sunshine, splendid restaurants — Menorca has something special. Such as dozens of lovely untouched beaches and a gorgeous countryside. And, as if that were not enough, it has the densest concentration of prehistoric monuments in Europe.

Although only small, much of the island is isolated and, without the help this book provides, difficult for the visitor to penetrate. Two days' driving will enable you to see most of that part of the island which is accessible by car (by no means all of it). As for the rest, it is gentle walking country, and the remoter regions are best explored on foot — or by bicycle.
— RODNEY ANSELL

Acknowledgements

Many thanks to the following people, who helped me with the preparation of earlier editions this book: Señora María Angeles Hernandez Gómez and her colleagues in the Ajuntament de Maó; Señor Lorenzo Cavallir; Sr Rafael Valls; Alan Goodin; Frankie and John Cross; and my wife, Helen. This Seventh edition, which has been updated by my publishers on the ground, not only incorporates many of the corrections and suggestions sent to Sunflower Books by users over the years but GPS tracks as well.

Useful books

Your library or local bookshop can suggest the best general guides prior to your departure. When you are on the island, you should be able to find the following reference books which I've found particularly helpful:

Joan Montserrat, Jaume Serrat *et al*, *Guide Menorca*

Hoskin and Waldren, *Taulas and Talayots*

Rev Fernando Marti, *History of Menorca*

M G Barredo, *Flowers of Menorca* and R Escandrell and S Catchot, *Birds of Menorca*; both of these can be purchased at the GOB bookshops in Maó (59 Camí d'Es Castell) and Ciutadella (38 Camí de Maó, only open Tuesdays 09.00-13.00 and Thursdays 10.00-14.00 and 17.00-20.00).

If you plan to walk the entire Camí de Cavalls, there are now several guides available and more coming out all the time, so best to search the web. You may not need it for route-finding, but a guide would be helpful for planning access and accommodation. There is a wealth of information on the web about the *camí*, and some sites offer interactive maps as well. See page 30 for more information about this round the island coastal walk.

If you enjoy using this book, and you would like to explore the countryside on another Balearic Island, Sunflower also publishes *Landscapes of Mallorca* and *Landscapes of Ibiza and Formentera*, again available from your usual map stockist or the web.

5

Introduction

How to get there

Menorca is easily reached by air to Maó airport. From May to October package holidays and 'flight only' arrangements from various airports throughout the UK are plentiful. There are also scheduled flights all year round — perhaps with EasyJet from Luton or Gatwick (the situation changes annually). Or fly with Iberia or Vueling via mainland Spain.

Geography

The island is small — only some 50km (30mi) by 20km (12mi) at its widest point. It is also a fairly flat island. There are low hills in the north, but no mountains. At 358m (1175ft), Monte Toro, in the centre of the island, is the highest point. This makes for generally easy walking.

The most significant geographical feature is the *cala*, the creek or fjord terminating in a tiny sandy beach. These lie at the end of the ravines, or *barrancs*, which cut through the southern half of the island particularly. Because of the many *barrancs,* the basic road pattern of Menorca is a central highway (the Me-1), from which arms branch off to the various beach resorts. There is no coastal road round the island, and circular drives are difficult to plan. (But there *is* a 'coastal road' for *walkers, cyclists and those on horseback* — see page 30.)

The vast majority of the population lives in five towns (Maó, Alaior, Es Mercadal, Ferreries and Ciutadella) strung across the centre of the island along the Me-1. Holidaymakers generally stay in a number of resorts dotted around the coast, mostly in the south and west. The rest of the island is given over to isolated farms, which connect with the road system and each other by rough tracks and, increasingly, newly-surfaced lanes — the setting for cycle trails and some of the walks detailed in this book. The fields, mostly used for dairy cattle, are separated by drystone walls. (It should not be difficult to climb over any walls on the walks in this book.)

Weather

July and August are hot and sunny. While there will be the occasional overcast or windy day, these will be infrequent. During spring, early summer and autumn, expect more cloudy days and rain. Menorca is the wettest of the Balearic Islands. It is the price paid for its gorgeous vegetation and abundant bird life. But it will not be cold, and there will be many hot and sunny days as well. A feature of the winter months is a strong, sometimes quite cold wind which at times blows from the north.

If you go to Menorca hoping to do some walking, the overcast days are a bonus — it is far more enjoyable walking then than in full sunshine — provided you have adequate protective clothing.

Where to stay

The bulk of the holiday accommodation is located in the beach resorts. There are plenty of hotels and apartments. Many people also stay in holiday villas. There is a shortage of domestic help: the population is small and — unlike much of Spain — fully employed. You will look in vain for signs of poverty. Very few hotels are open between November and April: search the web, ask a travel agent, or book direct with an owner to stay in a villa or apartment. There are **campsites** near Cala Galdana and Son Bou (see the touring map).

Getting about on the island

A frequent **bus service** plies between Maó and Ciutadella along the Me-1, calling at the three intervening towns where there are bus stops *(paradas fijas)* whose locations change regularly. The bus leaves Maó from the southwest side of the Plaça de S'Esplanada, and Ciutadella from the Plaça de la Pau, well south of the inner ring road. A less frequent service goes from Maó to Fornells via Arenal and Son Parc. The services to the beach resorts only operate in the summer. These link the southern resorts with Maó, and the northwestern ones with Ciutadella. Bus timetables are given on pages 133-134. Don't rely solely on these, however. Download the latest timetables from the bus operators' websites shown on page 133 or get 'first-hand' information from the bus stations mentioned above, the tourist offices, or the bus stops. Buses generally run to time but, to be on the safe side, always arrive about ten minutes early. Most of the walks in this book can be reached by bus. Not all walks will be convenient from your resort, but there will be some that are. A few walks can only be reached by car.

Taxis are only a phone call away should you miss your bus. If you use your mobile to make local calls in Menorca, you can take a **taxi** to the start of a walk and arrange where to be picked up when you call at the end of the walk. This enables you to do all those walks described as 'only accessible by car'. Your holiday rep, hotel reception and the tourist information offices in Ciutadella and Maó can all provide you with telephone numbers. The Asociació Menorquina de Radio-taxi operates an English-speaking 24 hour service (tel 971 36 71 11). All fares should be ascertained in advance.

Package tour couriers arrange **coach tours** which get you to all the tourist points of interest, but not off the beaten track.

Boat trips are also arranged by tour companies, or can be booked privately from Maó, Es Castell and Ciutadella harbours. These often provide a barbecue lunch at a beach.

Bicycles can be readily hired, and the countryside south of Ciutadella in particular lends itself to exploration in this way. Information about waymarked cycle trails (see the panel on page 84) is available from tourist offices. But be warned: the tarmac roads have a habit of turning into rough tracks — although these are ideal for mountain bikes!

Language hints

Out in the countryside, a few words of Spanish may be helpful, especially if you lose your way. Here's an (almost) foolproof way to communicate in Spanish. First, memorise the few short key questions and their possible answers, given below.

Then, when you have your 'mini-speech' memorised, *always ask the many questions you can concoct from it in such a way that you get a 'sí' (yes) or 'no' answer*. Never ask an open-ended question such as 'Where is the main road?' Instead, ask the question and suggest the most likely answer yourself. For instance: 'Good day, sir. Please — where is the path to Ferreries? Is it straight ahead?' Now, unless you get a 'sí' response, try: 'Is it to the left?'

If you go through the list of answers to your own question, you should eventually get a 'sí' response, and this is more reassuring than relying on sign language.

Following are the most likely situations in which you may have to practise your Spanish. The dots (...) show where you will fill in the name of your destination. Ask a local person — perhaps someone at your hotel — to help you with the pronunciation of place names.

■ Asking the way
Key questions

English	*Spanish*	*Pronunciation*
Good day	Buenos días	Boo-**eh**-nohs **dee**-ahs
sir (madam, miss)	señor (señora, señorita)	sen-**yor** (sen-**yor**-ah, sen-yor-**ee**-tah)
Please — where is	Por favor — dónde está	Poor fah-**vor** — **dohn**-day es-**tah**

English	Spanish	Pronunciation
the road to ... ?	la carretera a … ?	lah cah-reh-**teh**-rah ah… ?
the footpath to …?	la senda de … ?	lah **sen**-dah day … ?
the way to … ?	el camino a … ?	el cah-**mee**-noh ah … ?
the bus stop?	la parada?	lah pah-**rah**-dah?
Many thanks.	Muchas gracias.	**Moo**-chas **gra**-thee-ahs.

Possible answers

English	Spanish	Pronunciation
Is it here?	Está aquí?	es-**tah** ah- **kee**?
there?	allí?	ahl-**yee**?
straight ahead?	todo recto?	**toh**-doh rayk-toh?
behind?	detrás?	day-**tras**?
right?	a la derecha?	ah lah day-**ray**-chah?
left?	a la izquierda?	ah lah eeth-kee-**er**-dah?
above?	arriba?	ah-**ree**-bah?
below?	abajo?	ah-**bah**-hoh?

■ **Asking a taxi driver to take you somewhere and return for you, or asking a taxi to meet you at a certain place and time**

English	Spanish	Pronunciation
Please —	Por favor —	Poor fah-**vor** —
take us to …	llévanos a …	l-**yay**-vah-nohs ah …
and return	y venga buscarnos	ee **vain**-gah boos-**kar**-nohs
at (place) at (time)	a … a …*	ah (place) ah (time)*

*Point out the time on your watch.

Place names

The majority of place names on Menorca are the names of farms. Occasionally you will see the name written large across the façade of the house. Where a settlement of any kind has to be named, from talayotic village to *urbanización*, it invariably takes its name from the farm on whose land it lies.

Generally the names are old. Many go back to the days of the Moors and are in Arabic, but most are Menorquín, the old language of the island, derived from Catalan. Some are in modern Catalan, and a few in Spanish. Do not be surprised to see as many as three or four spellings for the same place — as at the farm of Son Mercer, visited on Walk 15.

A number of words occur again and again, and with the hope that it may add interest to your excursions, I offer below an explanation of the most frequent.

Firstly, however, some pronunciation hints are called for. In Menorquín 'ç' is pronounced as 's', 'll' as 'y' and 'x' as 'sh'. Here again, I do urge you to get some tips on pronunciation from a local person.

torre — a tower (sometimes corrupted to *turru* or *torr*). Menorca is full of towers, from prehistoric *talayots* to the watchtowers of the 17th and 18th centuries, by way of the fortified farmhouses of the Middle Ages, and a great many names include this element.

es, sa, ses — Menorquín equivalents of the Spanish *el, la, los/las. En, na* are variants of *es* and *sa*, used when referring to people, including names. All mean the same: 'the', as does *els* (Catalan) and *al* (Arabic).

san (Spanish), *sant* (Catalan), and *santa* (common to both Spanish and Catalan) mean saint: thus Sant Joan = San Juán = Saint John; Sant Jaume = San Jaime = Saint James.

cova or *cove* — a cave
cala — a creek or cove
barranc(o) — a gorge, river, or valley
son — a large farmhouse
bou — an ox
lloc, lluc — a Moorish word for a farmhouse

bini — a very common Moorish word meaning 'sons'
nou — new
vell (also *vella, vei, vey*) — old
de dalt — higher
de baix — lower
de devant — in front
de derrera — behind

The six above entries are usually found in pairs. As families grew, and the sons built their homes nearby, the new farms were distinguished in this way from the parents' farm.

In recent years there has been a strong revival of the Menorquín language. Many Spanish names of both towns and streets have been altered to Menorquín and/or Catalan, and many of the signs indicating public buildings, etc have also been revised. Some of the most common Menorquín words, with Spanish and English equivalents, follow:

Towns:

Maó — Mahón	Ciutadella — Ciudadela
Alaior — Alayor	Ferreries — Ferrerías
Es Migjorn (Gran) — San Cristobal	Sant Climent — San Clemente
Sant Lluís — San Luís	Es Castell — Villa-Carlos

Streets, etc:

carrer (calle) — street	costa (cuesta) — hill
plaça (plaza) — square	avinguda (avenida) — avenue
ajuntament (ayuntamiento) — town hall	mercat (mercado) — market
centre ciutat (centro ciudad) — city centre	platja (playa) — beach
	camí (camino) — road

Shops, etc:

obert (abierto) — open	tancat (cerrado) — closed

The name of the island:

The Romans called it Minorica, from which the English name Minorca was derived. It means the 'smaller' island (Majorca being the larger one). The Spanish equivalents are Menorca and Mallorca.

Country code

Experienced ramblers are used to following a country code; tourists perhaps less so. Please heed the following guidelines during your visit to Menorca.

- Do not light fires.
- Do not frighten animals.
- Walk quietly through all hamlets and villages.
- Leave all gates just as you find them.
- Protect all wild and cultivated plants. Don't try to pick wild

Walk 14: cows near Ferreries. Ever since Sir Richard Kane introduced British breeds of cattle, dairy farming has been an important agricultural activity on Menorca.

flowers or uproot saplings. Fruit and other crops are some-one's private property and should not be touched.
- Never walk over cultivated land (unless there is an explicit instruction to do so in the text, as in Walk 15).
- Take all your litter away with you.
- Walkers — Do not take risks! Do not attempt walks beyond your capacity, and do not wander off the paths described here, especially if it is late in the day. **Do not walk alone**, and *always* tell a responsible person exactly where you are going and what time you plan to return. Remember, if you become lost or injure yourself, it may be a long time before you are found. On any but a very short walk close to towns or villages, take some extra food, water, and warm clothing. A torch and whistle, even a compass, might be carried as well. *Do* read the guidelines on grade and equipment for each walk you plan.

PREHISTORIC MONUMENTS

Menorca is home to the greatest concentration of prehistoric monuments on earth. It is only recently that many of them have been excavated, restored, or cleared of the vegetation that for centuries had overwhelmed them. Very many more await excavation. Several of the walks in this book include visits to some of the most interesting of these monuments.

Talayot *at Talatí de Dalt*

The people of ancient Menorca worked with stone. The island is lacking in commercially useful metal ores, and there are no large trees for timber. Stone on the other hand abounds: south of a line drawn roughly from Cala Morell to Maó via Ferreries, a young and easily-worked limestone is found, which nevertheless becomes hard and durable when exposed to the atmosphere.

There are five principal kinds of building to be seen: caves, *talayots, taulas*, hypostyle chambers and *navetas*.

Capades de Moro at Cala Morell (Walk 23)

Caves *(illustrated above and on page 131)*

After 2500 BC the earliest inhabitants carved out caves for themselves to live in. Those who suppose that cavemen were primitive savages inhabiting natural holes in the cliffs will be totally unprepared for the sophisticated craftsmanship of these troglodytic homes, all of which were carefully and skillfully chiselled out of the rock. Later generations moved out of the caves between 1400 and 1000 BC, and for the next thousand years they were used only as burial chambers. While you will see caves on most walks, the best and easiest to explore will be found on Walks 2, 5, 11, 13, 17, 18, 19 and 22 and on Picnics 4, 11, 15, 16 and 18.

Talayots *(illustrated above and on pages 54-55, 60-61, 79)*

These great conical mounds of stones, 5-10m (15-30ft) high, are very common on the island. Many are solid; some have an inside chamber and passage. All are now truncated. Their original purpose is not known. Many suggestions have been made. Perhaps they had a timber house on top — for the local chieftain. Or they could have been defence towers, farmhouses, or storerooms. They are always associated with settlements. The best *talayots* are seen on Walks 2, 5, 7, 8, 12, 13, 17 and 21 and Picnics 5, 13, 21 and 22.

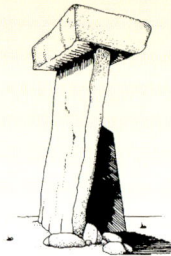

Taula *at Trepucó*

Taulas (illustrated on pages 1, 54-55 and opposite)

Most fascinating are the *taulas*, named from the Latin word *ta(b)ula* meaning 'table'. Whereas the *talayot* is not totally unlike buildings found elsewhere (the *nuraghe* of Sardinia for example), the *taula* is unique to Menorca.

It is a large, sometimes huge, slab of stone, set upright in a groove in the rock and supporting another large slab lying horizontally across it. The *taula* is always found in settlements, never far from a *talayot*, and inside a small horseshoe shaped enclosure, surrounded by standing stones, like a tiny Stonehenge.

Once again, nobody knows what they were for, and the ancient writers do not mention them. It is claimed they are too tall to be altars, and the most popular suggestion is that they are idols, like totem poles in North America, symbols of gods. One scholar has suggested that they may represent bulls' heads.

Most of the best *taulas* on the island are visited during Walks 2, 5, 7, 8 and 17 or Picnics 5, 13 and 21.

Hypostyle chambers (illustrated above right)

'Hypostyle chamber' describes a roof supported by pillars. These buildings, partly underground, are

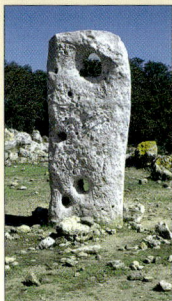

Excavation to the west of Trepucó

built up with large stones. They are roofed quite haphazardly with huge stones lying across the stone pillars, which are always much wider at the top than at the bottom.

Hypostyle chambers can be seen on Walks 2, 5, 7, 8, 13 (where one is still in use as an animal shed) and 15, as well as Picnics 5 and 13.

Hypostyle chamber at Torre d'en Galmés

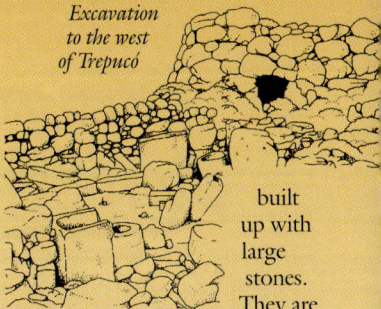

Left: standing stone at Talatí de Dalt; above right: naveta at Rafal Rubí

Navetas (illustrated above and on page 125)

So named in 1818 by Juán Ramis y Ramis, the first Spanish writer on Menorcan prehistory, the *naveta* is a stone-built burial chamber which resembles an upside-down boat. Hence its name, from the Latin word for boat *(navis)*. The *naveta* was always built some distance from the village. Two walks visit *navetas:* 8 and 21.

🌻 Short walks and picnicking

Menorca abounds in quiet, shady, isolated, scenic spots perfect for picnicking. All the car tours and walks in this book indicate several such ideal places. Unfortunately, many of them are only accessible on foot and are not very close to bus stops.

There are 22 picnic suggestions on the following pages. All are indicated on the touring map by the symbol *P* printed in green. However, as many of the picnics lie along or near the route of walks, you can pinpoint their location on the appropriate large-scale *walking* map, where you will also find the symbol *P*.

All the information you need to get to these picnics is given below; 🚌: how to get there by bus; 🚗: where to park your car. Please glance over the comments before you start off on your picnic: if some walking is involved, remember to wear sensible shoes and to take a sunhat (○ = picnic in full sun.) Take a plastic groundsheet as well, in case the ground is damp or prickly.

1 ERMITA DE SANT JOAN (Car tours 1 and 2, Walk 3; town plan pages 36-7 and map on reverse of touring map; photo page 45)

🚌 to Maó. Follow Shorter walk 3, allowing about 40min on foot.
🚗 From the roundabout at the junction of the Me-3 and Me-7 above the port, head south on the dual carriageway. Turn right after 50m, then immediately left on a minor road. Park at the church (0.8km/0.5mi). **No walking.**

2 CALA DE SANT ESTEVE (Car tour 1, Walk 4; map on reverse of touring map; nearby photo page 56)

🚌 to Es Castell; then follow notes for motorists below. **40min on foot.**

🚗 Drive from Maó past Es Castell. Keep straight on at the Sol del Este/Sant Lluís crossroads, and turn right just short of the army base along a narrow road. Follow the road round the *cala* and park at the end. Climb up beside an old tower to gain access to the coast, and picnic anywhere you like. Allow up to **10min on foot.** You will find some shade at the Torre d'en Penjat. (See also Picnic 17; it is close by.)

3 ES GRAU (Car tours 1 and 2, Walk 2; map page 41; photo of a similar setting page 42, top right)

🚌 from Maó to Es Grau; then see notes for motorists below.
🚗 Drive along the Fornells road

Climbing the old Roman road to Santa Agueda (Picnic 8; Car tour 2). See also notes in the panel on page 63.

(Me-7) from Maó and in 0.8km/0.5mi take the first road on the right for Es Grau. Park by the beach. There are two pine-shaded picnic places near this magnificent beach. One is among the trees which border the beach itself. For the second, allow up to **20min on foot**: walk to the end of the beach and follow the Camí de Cavalls up the cliff. Turn left at the top and descend to a little valley, where you will find an open space among trees. For a short walk, follow the *Camí* round to the right, up out of the valley, and turn right at the top, by a wall. Then follow the track back towards Es Grau (seen ahead). Turn right at a junction, go down into a valley, then climb steeply, to regain your outgoing route. Keep straight on, back to the beach.

4 CALA MORELL (*Car tour 2, Walk 22; map pages 126-7; photos on pages 12, 126*)

🚗 to Cala Morell; park in the car park on the right. The rocks may be too crowded, but the area around the caves, described in Walk 22 (page 128), should be quieter; up to **5min on foot**.

5 TALATI DE DALT (*Car tour 2, Walks 7 and 8; map on reverse of touring map; photos on pages 1, 13, 60-1*)

🚗 Leave Maó along the Me-1. In 4km turn south along a metalled lane, signposted to Talatí de Dalt, for 0.5km. Park in the parking area. The notes for Walks 7 and 8 tell you more about the site, usually quiet enough for a peaceful picnic. An entrance fee is payable.

6 CALA MESQUIDA (*Car tour 1; map on reverse of touring map*) ○

🚗 Park at the rear of the splendid, usually quiet, Cala Mesquida north of Maó. Picnic on the beach, or explore the cliffs.

7 CALA PRESILI (*Car tour 1; touring map*) ○

🚗 Drive from Maó towards Fornells along the Me-7, and turn right in 9km along a road signposted to Favàritx. Park at the end of the road, by the entrance to the lighthouse (at the KM2 marker). Allowing **20min on foot**, walk back 0.7km/0.5mi to the small 100m-marker with the number 3. Turn left here along a rocky track, and in seven minutes turn left at junction. Five minutes later you reach the small beach. (You could take a much longer walk here, following the waymarked Camí de Cavalls.)

8 SANTA AGUEDA (*Car tour 2; touring map; photo above*)

🚗 Turn north off the Me-1 some 3km northwest of Ferreries, towards the hill of Santa Agueda, and in 3km park beside the former village school. To the right of the school a gate gives onto a path, a Roman road, still partly paved. In **5min** you reach a quiet shady spot with stones to sit on; **30min** brings you to the top of the hill, where the Romans had a fortress and a Moorish king had his summer palace. Here too the Moors made their last stand against King Alfonso in 1287.

9 S'ARANGI (Car tour 1, Walk 24; map page 131, photos on pages 131 and 132) 🏕

🚗 Park as for Walk 24, page 131. A few shaded tables. **No walking**, or you could do Short walk 24.

10 CANTERA DE SANTA PONÇA (Car tour 1, map page 70-1)

🚌 to Alaior and walk *carefully* along the Me-1 to the parking place for motorists (about 1.5km from the petrol station in Alaior, see map); then follow notes for motorists below. Allow about **30min on foot**.

🚗 Park 1km west of the Alaior roundabout on the Me-1, in front of an electricity substation. Follow the access lane for Villa Tanus just west of the substation. After 500m, fork left on a rising concrete track, to the entrance to the quarries (**10min**). This is an astounding setting, with limestone walls 100m/300ft high and ample shade. If you like, follow the lane for another 1.2km, to some old army barracks on the left and ammunition caves on the right. The barracks have been vandalised and sprayed with graffiti, but their original rosy colouring is most attractive.

11 CALA MACARELLA (Car tour 2, Walks 17-9; map pages 94-95)

🚌 to Cala Santa Galdana, then follow notes for motorists below and allow **40min on foot**.
🚗 Drive to Cala Santa Galdana. On reaching the roundabout

outside the town, take the second exit to the bay; there is a large car park on the right. Now allow **40min on foot**. Follow the first section of Walk 18 from Cala Santa Galdana to Cala Macarella, using the notes on pages 102-103.

12 CALA PREGONDA (Car tours 1 and 2; touring map) ○

🚗 From the most northerly roundabout on the Es Mercadal ring road, take the exit for 'Platges Costa Nord' (brown sign). Turn right at the T-junction and, just before the next roundabout, take the slip road to the right, with another brown sign for 'Platges Costa Nord'. Follow this narrow country road, the Camí de Tramuntana, *past* a first road 2.5km along signposted right to Cala Pregonda and Binimel-là, but after 6.5km turn *sharp* right for Cala Pregonda and Binimel-là. After 0.5km turn left along a very wide dirt road, eventually forking left to the large parking area for Binimel-là beach and restaurant. Now allow **20-25min on foot**. From the parking area turn left on a track with barred vehicle access and a Camí de Cavalls information board at the left. Follow the well signed *Camí* through a gap in the wall here and then to the beach at Cala Pregonda.

13 TORRE TRENCADA (Car tour 2, Walks 17 and 21; map pages 94-5) 🏕

🚗 Coming from Ciutadella on the Me-1, turn right shortly before the KM39 marker along a country lane with a magenta signpost, 'Torretrencada'. Turn left at the T-junction, and after 2km park in a small car park. Follow the signposted path to the site of the prehistoric settlement of Torre Trencada (**8min on foot**), with its megalithic picnic table set beneath ancient olive trees in the middle of a prehistoric village.

14 CALO D'ES RAFALET (Car tour 1, Walk 12; map page 78, photo 76)

🚌 to S'Algar; then see notes for motorists below.

🚗 Drive to S'Algar. Turn right as you enter the resort, and park in the car park on your right. Allow **40min on foot**. Walk down to the seafront and turn left. At the end of the seafront, walk past a wall, turn left, and walk uphill beside it. Continue with the sea to your right, up to the top of the hill. Use the stile to climb over the wall here, turn left and walk parallel with the creek, to the end of a long field. Turn right, and go downhill to a gap in the wall. Cross another field to leave through the gap at the wall's end. Turn right along a track, and in 20m/yds turn right again. As the track turns left, look for a gap in the wall on your right after 20m/yds (waymarked with a red arrow on a tree). Turn right and follow the path along a dried-up river bed to the end, where you will find a shady picnic area. Follow the path on to a tiny sandy beach and lovely little cove.

15 CALES COVES from Cala'n Porter (Car tour 1; touring map)

🚌 to Cala'n Porter. From the bus stop allow **35min on foot**. Bear left and walk uphill along the main street to the cliff edge, following signs for the 'Cova d'en Xoroi'. Now refer to notes for motorists below.

🚗 Drive to Cala'n Porter. Do not take the road on the right down to the beach, but go straight through the town to the cliff edge. Park where convenient and allow about **15min on foot**. Turn left along the cliff edge, and follow any of the several paths parallel with the sea which is rarely more than 12m/yds away. In ten minutes you will be looking over the end of the creek. The path turns left here, parallel now with the *cala*. In about five minutes you will come to a place where you have a good view of the prehistoric caves in the cliffs opposite. Behind you the pine wood offers several open shady areas just right for picnicking on a hot day.

16 CALES COVES from Son Vitamina (Car tour 1; touring map) ○

🚌 Take the Cala'n Porter bus from Maó and alight at the Son Vitamina bus stop. Walk up the side road for 150m/yds to a roundabout; then see notes for motorists below.

🚗 Leave the Maó/Cala'n Porter road at the Cales Coves sign. Drive up the side road for 150m/yds to a roundabout. Just beyond it is a parking area. Walk back to the roundabout, bear left, then turn left down a track signposted 'Cales Coves' and allow **30min on foot**. Walk down the track on your right, to arrive at a picturesque creek in whose cliffs are many prehistoric caves.

17 FORT ST PHILIP (Car tour 1, Walk 4; map on reverse of touring map; photo page 49) ○

🚌 to Es Castell and **25min on foot**. Walk southeast beside the main road as far as the Sol del Este crossroads. Turn left and walk towards the sea. Now refer to notes for motorists below.

FLOWERS AND BIRDS

Menorca is wonderfully rich in wild flowers and birds. Although having the characteristic brown appearance of Mediterranean countries during July and August, for most of the year the island's ample rainfall gives it a rich green colouring, splashed with the vivid hues of its multitude of flowers.

Left to itself, I suppose that the mastic bush, *Pistacia lentiscus*, would soon take over the whole island. You will see it everywhere — growing out of walls and blocking footpaths you want to use, covering *talayots*, trapped behind stone walls in the middle of every field. There are many other bushes and shrubs to be found, including myrtle and juniper, wild olive and fig, but very few trees. The pine is the only common real tree, especially *Pinus halepensis*, the Aleppo pine, although *Pinus pinea*, the umbrella pine, is also to be found. Mercifully the bushes are more or less contained, allowing such a variety of wayside flowers to flourish as to excite wonder and envy in the English visitor. Over a thousand species of plant have been identified on the island, and what is in flower will depend on the month of your visit. In early summer the gardener whose pride is in his gladioli will certainly see *Gladiolus communis*, its wild ancestor. Widespread and spectacular is *Hedysarum coronarium*, with red lupin-like flowers. In the same season you will see everywhere asphodel with white flowers raised high on long stems above yucca-like leaves. The pasture fields are filled with varie-gated thistles and walls festooned with pink *Convolvulus althaeoides*, wild roses and *Cistus*. Common 'weeds' of the verges are the herb fennel, whose feathery leaves smell of aniseed, and vivid red poppies. October sees the autumn crocus whose delight is to push through the bare earth of the tracks you walk along.

In high summer the flowers are dead, but the withered seed heads of this multitude of plants feed an equal abundance of birds at this time, none more prolific than the goldfinch, while in spring and early summer the song of birds is unending wherever you walk.

The national bird is the red kite. It is unmistakable, and rarely will you complete a walk without one slowly circling above your head. It is a very large bird, with wings ending in 'fingers' spread wide. From below, silhouetted, the large white patches under its wings and its deeply forked tail make it easy to identify. Seen from above when it swoops into a valley, the sun blazing down upon it, it is magnificent.

Most large white birds circling round pretending to be hawks will be herring gulls. You will always know when a fishing boat is coming in by the cloud of herring gulls above it.

But if you spot a huge white bird of prey with black flight feathers, straw-coloured head and and diamond-shaped tail, you are having the good fortune to be looking at an Egyptian vulture.

If you're walking here in spring or autumn, all the little birds you see seem to have black heads and pale bellies. This is because it is a characteristic of four very common species: blackcap, Sardinian warbler, stonechat and pied flycatcher (this last a passage migrant in April, September and October). The stonechat is probably the easiest of the four to pick out. His back is black as well

Continued on page 103

🚗 Drive from Maó past Es Castell as far as the Sol del Este cross-roads. Turn left and park just before the road bends left. Now allow **5min on foot**. Follow the road round to the left and on for 100m/yds, as far as the Cafetería Sol del Este. Turn right beyond it down an unnamed passage, to the coastal path at the end. Turn right to reach a wall with a stile, which gives you access to the site of Fort St Philip and a superb picnic spot where you can watch the cruise liners in the harbour. There are exceptional views of the harbour mouth, Sa Mola and the Illa del Llatzeret. Explore the remains of Fort St Philip as far as the *zona militar*. (Note that Picnic 2 is nearby, on the south side of St Stephen's Creek.)

18 SON BOU (Car tour 2, Walk 11; map pages 72-3; photos pages 73 and 74) 🏞

🚐 to Son Bou. Walk down the road towards the beach; then see notes for motorists below. **2min on foot.**
🚗 to Son Bou. Park in the car park beside the beach, and leave by the entrance you drove in. As you turn towards the beach you will see in front of you a well-appointed pine-shaded picnic site with benches and tables. **No walking.**

19 CALA DE ALGAIARENS (Walk 22; map page 126-7, photo page 30)

🚗 Head from Ciutadella to Cala Morell, but when the Cala Morell road turns left, keep straight on for 3km to the turn-off left. Ignore the first car park on the right; continue to a second car park, just past a signboard for the Camí de Cavalls on the right. There are shaded picnic tables, toilets, and a wonderful beach. **No walking** or

follow the 'Short circuit' described on page 128.

20 CALA SON SAURA (Walk 18; map page 99 and touring map)

🚗 Leave Ciutadella on the Cala'n Turqueta road, but fork right after 3km on a good road. In 3km you will pass the 'poblat', or prehistoric village, of Son Catlar and in a further 2km arrive at the gateway to the Torre Saura Vell estate, where you will pay a parking fee. Drive 2km along a fairly good farm track to a car park. There are shaded picnic tables beyond the car park as well as a fabulous beach. **No walking**.

21 SON CATLAR (touring map)

🚗 Leave Ciutadella on the Cala'n Turqueta road, but fork right after 3km on a good road. In 3km you will come to the 'poblat', or prehistoric village, of Son Catlar. It is maintained by the same group of archaeological enthusiasts that looks after Talatí de Dalt (the site of Picnic 5). There is a large car park. The prehistoric village is completely enclosed by its original wall, all 870m/yds of it. There is plenty of shade. Expect to pay an entrance fee. **Very short walk**.

22 TORRE LLAFUDA (Car tour 2; touring map)

🚗 A short way west of the km37 marker on the Me-1 there is a magenta sign beside the lane leading to Son Sintes farm announcing 'Torrellafuda'. Turn here and drive along the lane for 0.8km/0.5mi. There is a car park and a small but very pretty *poblat* or prehistoric village with *talayot*, *taulas* and burial caves. It is usually quiet and there is plenty of shade. **No walking**.

☀ Touring

There are many car hire firms on Menorca, or you can reserve a car via your travel agent or holiday company at home. Charges can vary considerably, so shop around. The cheapest deal does not necessarily mean the worst car. Be certain to ask for and get 'Collision Damage Waiver', otherwise you will be liable for any repair bill for the car that you incur. On which topic, a word of warning. If you are only used to right-hand drive cars and driving on the left, then collecting your totally unfamiliar car at the airport, after dark, can be un-nerving — especially if you had a few drinks on the flight … making you illegally over the limit.

Always check your vehicle in advance and point out any existing dents, scratches etc. Ask for all the conditions and insurance cover in writing, in English. Check to make sure you have a sound spare tyre and all the necessary tools. Be sure to get the office and the after-hours telephone numbers of the hire firm and carry them with you. If you are not 100% happy with the car, don't take it. Finally, if you pay by credit card, make a note of exactly what you are signing for.

The two car tours will take you to the majority of the notable places on the island (indicated with a ★ in the touring notes and on the touring map). The touring notes are quite brief. I concentrate on the 'logistics' of touring and the possibilities for nearby **countryside picnics** and **walks**. (Usually further historical notes can be found in the text with the relevant walk or in the boxed panels listed on page 4.)

The large fold-out touring map is designed to be held out opposite the touring notes and contains all the information you will need outside the towns. Town plans of Maó and Ciutadella, showing exits for motorists, are on pages 36-37 and 110-111 respectively. Notice the walking areas marked out in dark green on the touring map: you may like to refer to these *walking maps* when touring — especially the one on the reverse of the touring map: they are at a much larger scale, with more detail.

Remember to allow plenty of time for visits. The times given in the tours are actual driving times, and no allowance has been made for time spent sightseeing. The distances quoted in the notes are *cumulative kilometres* from the departure point. A key **to the symbols** used in the touring notes is on the touring map.

Car tour 1: EASTERN MENORCA

Maó/Mahón • Favàritx • Arenal d'en Castell • Fornells • Es Mercadal • Monte Toro • Alaior • Torralba • Cala'n Porter • (Cales Coves) • Sant Climent • Binibèquer Vell • Sant Lluís • Es Castell • Maó/Mahón

129km/81mi; about 4 hours' driving
On route: Picnics (see pages 14-19) 1, 2, 3, 6, 7, 9, 12, 14, 15, 16, 17; Walks 1, 2, 3, 4, 5, 6, 7, 8, 9, 10, 12
The roads are generally good and adequately wide, although occasion- *ally bumpy. There are petrol stations in Maó, on the Me-7 two kilometres before the Arenal turn-off, and in Alaior.* **Important**: *although the driving time is only four hours, allow an entire day if you want to visit all the tourist attractions.*

A modern highway, the Me-1, runs across Menorca connecting the capital Maó/Mahón with the second largest town and former capital, Ciutadella. On it lie the three next largest towns of the island — Alaior, Es Mercadal and Ferreries. Just outside Maó on this road there is a large oval roundabout, which has been taken as the nominal start and finish of this tour, although being circular it can be joined and left wherever is convenient.

Coming from **Maó★** (✝🏔🏠⚓✕🚇 ⌨**M**; Walks 1, 3, 5-7; notes page 33), turn right at the roundabout and follow the dual carriageway downhill towards the port. At the bottom of the hill take the third exit from the roundabout, the Me-7 signposted to Fornells and Es Grau (the second exit, the Me-3, leads to Cala Mesquida; Picnic 6). This is the beginning of the Camí d'en Kane (Kane's Road), built early in the 18th century by the first British lieutenant-governor of Menorca, Sir Richard Kane, to link Ciutadella in the north with Port Maó, replacing the earlier road built by the Romans. You will see a memorial to him on your right soon after the start of the road. This first stretch necessitated the draining of marshes, resulting in the creation of the rich agricultural land on your left. Some 180m past the monument, turning left and left again (over a bridge) on the Camí de Baix de Sant Joan would take you to the setting for Picnic 1 and Walk 3.

Almost at once pass the Me-5 on the right to Es Grau★, a tiny resort with a large beach (Picnic 3, Walk 2). Soon the Camí d'en Kane bears away to the left. However you keep straight on along the Me-7, following signs for Fornells. The road continues in a north-westerly direction through a beautiful countryside of lightly-wooded low hills. Just 2.9km beyond the Camí d'en Kane turning, the track in front of the lovely Biniarroca estate on the left leads to Walk 9c. Continue towards Fornells for somewhat over a kilometre, when you will pass on your right a little church on a wooded hill, the Ermita de Fátima.

Another road now goes to the right, signposted to Favàritx. Turn along here. At first the road (Cf-1) is very straight as it crosses flat terrain, passing the Capifort estate, before winding between low green

21

hills, to end at the lighthouse at **Cape Favàritx**, shown on the cover of the book (17.5km). There is car parking here and, 0.7km back along the road, a track on the left brings you in 12 minutes' walking to the beach of Cala Presili (Picnic 7). Perhaps you will return another day and try a hike along the Camí de Cavalls (see page 30) which runs both west and south from the lighthouse.

Returning to the Me-7, turn right to drive through increasingly wooded scenery. In 6.5km you come to a roundabout. Three resorts lie at the end of the road to the right: Arenal d'en Castell, Na Macaret and Port d'Addaia. Arenal probably has the most to offer you, although Port d'Addaia can provide a boat trip along a charming *cala*, the third longest in Menorca. All three are well signposted: turn right on the Me-9 and, when you come to a cross-roads, go left for Arenal, straight on for Na Macaret, or right for Addaia. The long, curved beach at **Arenal d'en Castell** (36km ▲▲✕) is one of the best on the island (*arenal* means 'sandy beach'). The small seaside village of Na Macaret (▲✕) is one of the oldest holiday resorts on Menorca. Port d'Addaia (▲✕) overlooks the harbour. When in the mid-18th century John Armstrong wrote the first English guide to Menorca, he described Addaia as the most exquisite place on the island.

Again return to the Me-7, turn right and follow signs for Fornells. In 3km you will pass the turn-off right for Son Parc★ (▲✕♿); its sandy beach, shown on page 129, is the goal of Walk 23. After 5.5km you pass the starting point for Walk 23 and 1km further on come to another roundabout at the junction with the Me-15. Turn right. For 4km the road runs beside the second largest *cala* on Menorca. Remote from Ciutadella and Maó, it was once a favourite anchorage of Mediterranean pirates. As a result no Menorcans would live there. In 1591 the governor decided that the time had come to do something about the pirates, and a start was made on fortifying the entrance to the harbour. The ruins of that fortress are seen if you walk towards the harbour mouth. Under its protection the lovely fishing village of **Fornells**★ (51km ♦▲✕📷; photo below) grew up. You can see on the Isla Sarganta in the bay a tower built by the British to provide crossfire and, on the headland overlooking the village and harbour entrance, a second tower.

Drive back beside the *cala* to the roundabout, then take the first

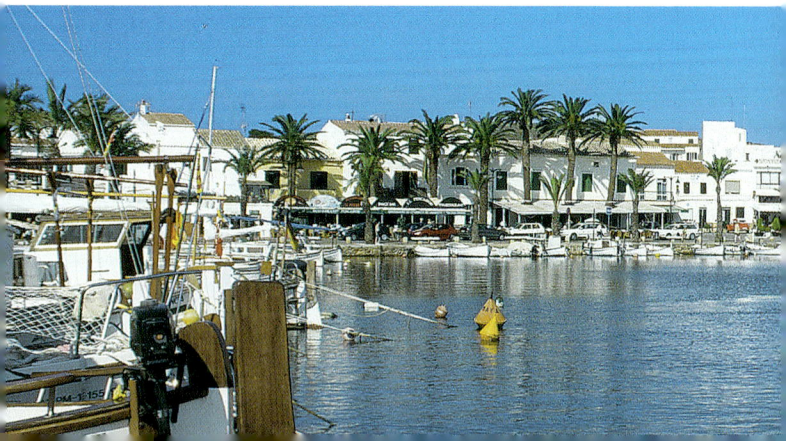

exit, a country lane signposted to Binimel-là. After 2km you pass a road off right to Cala Tirant. Two kilometres further on I recommend that you turn right for 'Cap' and 'Far' de Cavallería. Some 4km along this road you pass the Roman site of Nitja and 3km further on come to the **Far de Cavallería** (M), where a small museum of the environment replaces an earlier eco-museum by Nitja (which closed for lack of funding).

After the detour, return to this junction and turn right. In 2km you will pass on your right the wide dirt road to the beach of Binimel-là (the turn-off for Picnic 12). Just over 0.4km further on, turn sharp left for Es Mercadal. Coming to a roundabout in just under 7km, take the third exit into 'Es Mercadal' (66km ♣♠✖M). After 250m turn left to a roundabout on the ring road. Take the second exit and the last exit at the next roundabout (with a magenta sign, 'Santuari del Toro'. A short, steep, winding drive leads to the summit★ of **Monte Toro** (69km ♣✖☞M; photos on page 69). At 358m/1175ft, this is the highest point on Menorca, from where the whole island can be seen. It is also the high point of Walk 10.

Its name probably dates back to the time of the Moorish occupation, deriving from the Arabic word *tor* meaning 'mountain'. However the fact that *toro* means 'bull' in Spanish has caused a curious legend to arise. It is claimed that the bull in question hewed with its horns a statue of the Virgin Mary out of rock, and that the name of the mountain commemorates this miracle.

Return to Es Mercadal and turn left at the roundabout. Take the second exit at the next roundabout, the Me-1 towards Maó. Shortly after leaving the town you will pass the electricity substation on the right, and then at the top of the hill you will find a viewpoint on the left looking out to the **Penya de s'Indi** (☎), the rock shown on page 131, which bears an uncanny resemblance to a Hollywood Red Indian chief. Walk 24 circles this rock; it begins 200m south of the viewpoint at the **Finca pública s'Arangí** (Picnic 9).

I highly recommend a short walk to the setting for Picnic 10: you pass the lane about 750m short of the Alaior bypass. Ignore the bypass and bear left to drive through **Alaior** (80km ♣✖🏪M;

Once a fishing village, Fornells (Car tour 1) is now the most chic resort on the island, visited by Spanish royalty.

notes in Walk 10). Just before the end of the town, at the traffic lights, turn right for 'Cala En Porter'. After 3km you will arrive at the important megalithic site of **Torralba d'en Salort**★ (83km **Ⓣ**; Walk 8). The road then bends right and passes close to two more important sites (**Ⓣ**), Torrellisa and So na Caçana, before reaching a roundabout on the Me-12 after 3.5km.

Turn right here and you will shortly arrive at **Cala'n Porter** (91.5km **▲▲▲✕▣**; Picnic 15). The fairly large holiday resort is built high above a fine beach. Set in the cliff at the end of the *cala* is the **Cave of Xoroi**★, a bar and nightclub built in a prehistoric cave dwelling. From Cala'n Porter follow the Me-12 east, back to the Alaior roundabout and then towards Sant Climent and Maó★.

At the roundabout at the end of **Sant Climent** (98.5km **✕**), turn right for 'Es Canutells'. Notice the stone seats along the walls on the left. They were made to accommodate spectators of the trotting races, still popular in Menorca, which were once held along here. In 2.5km pass a road off right to Cala Canutells and keep straight on to **Binidalí**, then turn left before you reach the sea.

It is impossible to give detailed directions for the next section of the tour: there are so many tiny

---

*But if you have time for a short walk (30min-1h return), 0.5km past the roundabout turn right for 'Calescoves' (magenta sign) at the next roundabout. Park about 1.5km along the track, before it becomes too rutted and walk down to the head of one of the prettiest of all the *calas* (**▲▲▲✕**) and the impressive troglodytic site of Cales Coves★ (**Ⓣ▣**; Picnic 16).

streets as you drive from one resort to the next. It scarcely matters; you cannot get lost. Just keep heading southeast, as close to the coast as you can, following signs for Cap d'en Font, Binissafúller, Binibèquer, Biniancola and Punta Prima — which you will pass during the next 10.5km.

One resort worth exploring is **Binibèquer Vell**★ (**▲✕▣**). It was one of the first *urbanizaciones* and was designed to replicate a typical Menorcan fishing village (a curious conceit, since there is no such thing; you have already seen Menorca's only fishing village — Fornells — and it is nothing like this!). At the southeast tip of the island is **Punta Prima** (113km **▲▲▲✕**). Here you turn left and head for Sant Lluís, some 5km distant. Halfway along, the Me-8 on the right leads to S'Algar and Picnic 14.

More about **Sant Lluís**★ (118.5 **ⓘ▲▲✕▣M**) can be read in Walk 12, which begins here. On leaving, turn right on the Me-6 for Es Castell. As you pass the village of Trebalúger on the right, look for its prominent *talayot*. In 4km you reach a crossroads near a cemetery. Until 1782 the road to the right led to the mighty Fort St Philip. Take it now for Picnic 2 or cross over for Picnic 17; otherwise turn left and skirt to the left of **Es Castell** (123km **ⓘ▲▲▲✕▣M**; notes in Walk 4). The road dips to Cala Figuera. Head right downhill. Turn left and drive the full length of Maó's harbour. At the end, turn left at the roundabout, up to the next roundabout in **Maó** (129km), where the tour began.

Car tour 2: WESTERN MENORCA

Ciutadella • Cala Santa Galdana • Es Migjorn Gran • Sant Tomàs • Sant Jaume Mediterrani • Alaior • Maó • Es Grau • Es Mercadal • Ferreries • Ciutadella

Distance: 152km/94mi; about 4 hours' driving
On route: Picnics (see pages 14-19) 1, 3, 4, 5, 8, 10, 11, 12, 13, 18, 22; Walks 2, 3, 7, 8, 11, 13, 14, 15, 16, 17, 18, 19, 20, 21, 22 *The roads are generally adequately wide and well surfaced. There are* *petrol stations in Ciutadella, Alaior, and just outside Es Mercadal. Note that there is a speed restriction on the Camí d'en Kane.* **Important:** *although the driving time is only four hours, allow a full day to visit all the tourist attractions.*

The ancient and fascinating city of Ciutadella has been chosen as the starting point of this tour, keeping in mind the many tourists based in the northwest of the island. Since the tour is circular it can, of course, be joined and left wherever convenient.

Ciutadella★ (†🏔🏔⛱✕➤📷M), starting point for Walks 20 and 21, is described in more detail on page 113. Leave the town along the Camí de Maó, the beginning of the Me-1 highway to Maó. After 4km look out for the **Naveta d'es Tudons★** (𝗧) on your right. It is clearly sign-posted and there is ample parking. A visit to this monu-ment is *de rigueur*, if only because of its claim to be the oldest roofed building in Europe. It can be visited on a variation of Walk 21, and you can read more about it on page 121.

At 5.3km turn right along a road signposted to **Torre Trencada** (magenta sign) and turn left at the crossroads in front of the Binigarba farm. Leave your car in the small parking area, and follow the path to the interesting prehistoric settle-ment visited on Walks 17 and 21 and Picnic 13. Then return to the Me-1 and

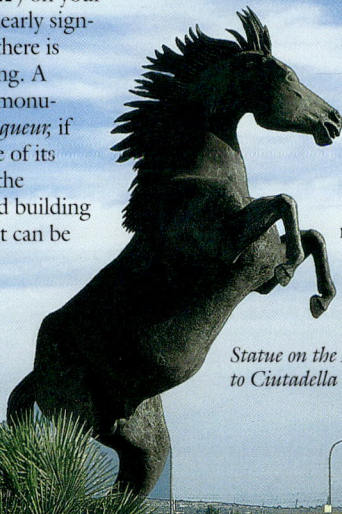

Statue on the Me-1 at the entrance to Ciutadella

turn right. In 2km, a lane on the right leads to yet another important prehistoric site, that of Torre Llafuda (**𝍏**; Picnic 22). Just over 5km further along, a lilac sign on the left signals a possible detour up a minor road, towards a hill with famous historical associations — Santa Agueda (264m/870ft; **𝍏☞**). A short walk would take you to the settings for Picnic 8.

The main tour continues on the Me-1 towards Ferreries. In 2.5km, at a roundabout, take the second exit to beautiful **Cala Santa Galdana**★ (29km **▲▲◆✕☞**; photo on page 96; Picnics 10 and 11, Walks 16-18; Shorter walk 19). When you reach the round-about at the resort's entrance, take the last exit signposted 'Mirador de sa Punta' and drive (past the starting point for Walk 16) to the end, where a walkway leads to a panoramic view over the bay.

Back on the Me-1, turn right towards Ferreries. In 0.5km, at the entrance to Ferreries, turn right along the Me-20 to **Es Migjorn Gran** (44.5km **✝◆✕**), a small town founded in 1763. Turn right on the far side of town, passing through a region rich in megalithic monuments (mostly not visible from the road). The road (Me-18) ends at a long silver-sand beach, at **Sant Tomàs**★ (48.5km **▲▲◆✕**; Walks 11, 13 and the extensions to Walk 16).

Return to Es Migjorn and keep straight ahead on the Me-18 towards Es Mercadal. In 3km, at a roundabout, turn right on the Me-16 towards Maó and Alaior. In 4km you rejoin the Me-1. Turn right and, after 1km, take the next road on the right, signposted (at time of writing) to 'Torre-Soli Nou'. Follow it down to **Sant Jaume Mediterrani**★ (66.5km

𝍏▲▲◆✕). It has a long beach separated from lines of villas by a wide marsh. At the roundabout at the entrance to the resort, take the second exit ('Farmacía, Centro Médico, Son Bou Scuba'). Ignore all roads to the left. At the 'Stop' sign in front of the marsh, turn left. Pass the bus stop and, at a roundabout in **Son Bou** (**✝**), turn right for the beach and car park (Picnic 18). Walk 11 starts here, and in the notes you can read more about the area, illustrated on pages 73 and 74.

Return to the roundabout, turn right and head towards Alaior. After somewhat over 4km turn right (magenta sign) and, in under 2km, keep left at a fork, to reach the largest of the cyclopean town-ships, **Torre d'en Galmés**★ (74km **𝍏**; drawing on page 13).

Drive back to the Son Bou/ Alaior road and turn right. In 2.5km you will be back at the Me-1 just as it reaches **Alaior** (79km **✝✕⊟M**), the third largest town on Menorca. If you wish to see it, drive straight under the bypass for 'Alaior', then follow 'Alaior' at the roundabout. Drive almost to the far side of the town where, at traffic lights, you will see a road on the right signposted 'Cala En Porter'. If you drive a short distance along here, you should find room to park beside the road. Walks 8 and 10 start here, and the notes for Walk 10 will tell you a little about the town.

Otherwise carry on along the Me-1 bypass, heading for Maó. On the way you will pass four *navetas:* two on the right at L'Argentina, and two on the left at Rafal Rubí (all indicated with magenta signposts). After 8km turn right on a minor road to the prehistoric site of **Talatí de Dalt**★ (87.5km

Cala Mitjaneta, with Cala Mitjana beyond it (Walk 16 from Cala Santa Galdana)

⚓; Picnic 5; Walks 7 and 8; notes on page 60; photos on pages 1, 12-13 and 60-61).

Returning to the main road, continue *past* the industrial estate to a large oval roundabout in **Maó** (the city is described on page 33). Turn left on the dual carriageway towards the port, and left again at the roundabout at the bottom of the hill.* In 0.7km take the Me-5 road on the right to **Es Grau★** (100km 🏠✕; Picnic 3; Walks 2a and 2b), a charming resort with a large and attractive beach. Heading back, turn right 2.5km south of Es Grau, for the 'S'Albufera Parc Natural', focal point of the island's biosphere reserve and a mecca for bird-watchers (Walk 2c).

*Circling this roundabout completely you can reach the Ermita de Sant Joan (Picnic 1 and Walk 3; photograph page 45); see Picnic 1 notes on page 14.

Go back to the Me-7 and turn right towards Fornells but, after 1.5km, turn left along the Camí d'en Kane. This road, described in Walk 3, affords pleasant driving through a rural landscape north of Alaior. Rejoin the Me-1 at a roundabout with the Es Mercadal bypass and follow signs for Ferreries and Ciutadella. Turning right here leads to Picnic 12. Both **Es Mercadal** (128km 🚻🏠✕M) and Ferreries are market towns founded after the Reconquest. Approaching **Ferreries** (136km 🚻🏠✕🚌M), *keep right under the ring road*, to follow the main road through the town. You pass a minor road on the right which is on the route of Walk 14; like Walk 15, it starts in Ferreries. Arriving back at back at **Ciutadella** (152km), you have the easiest access to Walks 19 and 22, as well as Picnics 4 and 19-21.

Walking

The walks in this book cover a good cross-section of the island. I have tried to choose walks which take you to places of interest. In some cases that will be historical or archaeological. In others it may be a beautiful, remote beach. There are walks to suit every taste from short strolls to rambles over 20 kilometres long. For a selection of *very* short walks, see the picnic suggestions on pages 14 to 19.

To choose a walk that appeals to you, you might begin by looking at the touring map inside the back cover. Here you can see at a glance the overall terrain, the roads, and the location of the walks. Flipping through the book, you will see that there is at least one photograph for every walk. Having selected one or two potential excursions from the map and the photos, turn to the relevant walk. At the top of the page you will find planning information.

Grading, waymarking, maps, GPS

The walks are **graded** according to distance, amount of ascent and roughness of the going underfoot. As is clear in the introduction, Menorcan terrain is mostly gentle, and there are only two grades assigned to these walks: easy (● gentle ascents/descents, easily followed); moderate (● more strenuous ascents/descents; variable surfaces underfoot).

Many routes in this guide follow the well-**waymarked** Camí de Cavalls; see page 30.

The large-scale (1:40,000) topo **maps**, based on Spanish Military maps but updated in the field with GPS, have been annotated to show important landmarks.

Free **GPS tracks** are available for all these walks: see the Menorca page on the Sunflower website. Please bear in mind, however, that GPS readings should *never* be relied upon as your sole reference point. Conditions can change at any time.

What to take

I recommend well worn-in **walking boots**, for the protection they give to the ankles, or **sports sandals** for summer. Beach sandals are *not* suitable for walking.

In summer you will need a long-sleeved shirt for **protection against the sun**, and for the same reason a sunhat and long trousers. If the walk includes a beach — and many do — take a towel, swimwear and suncream. Have **water-**

COTO PRIVADO DE CAZA

Most fields in Menorca are marked with one or other of two warning notices. One is *Coto Privado de Caza*. It means 'Private Shooting' ie the right to shoot game on the property is reserved to the owner of the land, or to whomsoever he may choose to rent out the right. Its equivalent here is the alternative notice, a rectangle divided diagonally into black and white triangles. The warning carries two implications: one is that you must not attempt to shoot game on the property. The other is that it would not be wise to stray from the marked path! The presence of occasional shotgun cartridges will confirm this. On Walk 10 you will see a happier notice: *Refugí de caça* (Game sanctuary).

proof clothing if it looks like rain, especially outside summer. You will need **water** and a **small rucksack** with a **first-aid kit** (including pain killers and plasters). A **whistle** and **torch** are always advisable.

Carry up-to-date **bus timetables** and of course your **smartphone or mobile** — for emergencies (112 is the emergency number throughout the EU) … to double-check where you are on a map or GPS … or just to call a taxi if the bus times don't work for you (see taxi details on pages 7-8). Bird-lovers should try to have lightweight **binoculars**. Use your good judgement to modify my list according to the season!

Nuisances

While there are large **dogs** on the island, they are almost always tied up. A few small dogs, not tied up, may continue to bark until they have seen you off their patch. If dogs worry you, buy an ultrasonic 'Dog Dazer' from one of the retailers on the web. The few **snakes** on the island are also harmless. You may come across **mountainbikers** on some trails or **jeep safaris** — or **quad bikes** — throwing up dust.

The walking notes

When you are on your walk, you will find that the text begins with an introduction and then turns to a description of the route. *Do compare your pace with mine* on one of the short walks, before taking a long hike. *Remember, the time checks are from one point to the next and do not take into account any stops at all.* Below is a key to the symbols on the maps.

═══	dual carriageway		— 200 —	height (metres)		P	picnic place (see pages 14-19)
═══	main road		🚌	bus stop			
═══	secondary road		🚗	car parking		∩✕	cave.quarry
═══	minor road		📷	best views		○	threshing floor
▨▨▨	cart/jeep track; dirt road		🏓	picnic tables		■☗	building.fortified
-------	footpath.steps		✚✚	church.chapel		🔲4	watchtower.waypoint
→→→	main walk		⊞	cemetery		⊗✗	stadium. windmill
→→→	alternative walk		⫪	prehistoric site		⊞	page reference

29

CAMI DE CAVALLS

Consequent on the blockhouses (see page 97) and watchtowers (page 105) was the need to be able to get soldiers to and from them. So from early times there existed a road more or less following the perimeter of the island. It is mentioned in literature dating from the 16th century, and came into prominence during the time of the British and French occupations of the 18th century.

In fact archives in Maó record that the first British lieutenant-governor, Sir Richard Kane, ordered the 'old King's Road around the coast to be marked out in March of every year with closely-spaced fresh green branches, the cost of this work to be born by the landowners through whose territory the road passes'. Moreover, 'where the road runs some distance inland, it should be re-routed closer to the coast — provided that the new route would be safe for travellers on horseback'.

This coastal road is known in Catalan as the 'Camí de Cavalls' (bridle-road). It was last used during the Spanish Civil War (1936-9), when the Republicans ordered it to be cleared ready for

use, with all landowners' obstructions removed. But at the end of the war it fell into disuse and became so overgrown that in places it could not even be identified. Other parts fell under tarmac through housing developments. But one of the major obstacles for those who tried to follow the *Camí* were the many obstacles put in their way by land-owners — as users of earlier editions of this guide found to their cost!

In the late 1990s a group of Menorcans formed a society to 'defend' the *Camí*. This pressure group succeeded in having an act passed by the Balearic Parliament in 2000 guaranteeing the reinstatement of the road for the benefit of walkers, cyclists and riders. It took years of negotiations with land-owners and clearance projects, but now the *Camí* is fully open and even has its own European long-distance path number: GR 223.

There are 20 stages, running counter-clockwise from Maó:

1 Maó–Es Grau (10km/3.5h, medium)

2 Es Grau–Favàritx (8.6km/3.5h, medium)

3 Favàritx–Arenal d'en Castell (13.6km/5h, medium)

4 Arenal d'en Castell–Cala Tirant (10.8km/4h, easy)

5 Cala Tirant–Binimel·là (9.6km/4h, medium)

6 Binimel·là–Els Alocs (8.9km/6h, difficult)

7 Els Alocs–Algaiarens (9.7km/4.5h, medium)

8 Algaiarens–Cala Morell (5.4km/2.25h, medium)

9 Cala Morell–Punta Nati (7km/3h, easy)

10 Punta Nati–Ciutadella (10.5km/4h, easy)

11 Ciutadella–Cap d'Artrutx (13.2/5h, easy)

12 Cap d'Artrutx–Cala d'en Turqueta (13.3km/5h, medium)

13 Cala d'en Turqueta– Cala Galdana (6.4km/2.5h, easy)

14 Cala Galdana–Sant Tomàs (10.8km/4.5h, medium)

15 Sant Tomàs–Son Bou (6.4km/2.5h, easy)

16 Son Bou–Cala en Porter (8km/3.5h, medium)

17 Cala en Porter– Binissafúller (11.8km/4.5h, easy)

18 Binissafúller–Punta Prima (8.1km/3.5h, easy)

19 Punta Prima–Cala de Sant Esteve (7.3km/2.75h, easy)

20 Cala de Sant Esteve– Maó (6km/2.25h, easy)

The stages are outlined in various books available from your usual map stockist or on the web. (The clearest map of the whole route is that published by Editorial Alpina at a scale of 1:50,000.) As usual, this Sunflower guide confines itself to day walks, but we include many sections of the *Camí*.

The clearing and maintaining of the trail, with some 3500 markers, represents a huge investment on the part of the island government. There are large signboards at either end of each stage, fingerposts at intersections, and stout, numbered wooden posts at 100m intervals in some rural areas — difficult to get lost! In urban areas the trail is marked by red/white flashes on street furniture.

And the government have not just confined themselves to the *Camí*: Walks 2b and c and Walk 24 use other official trails opened since earlier editions of this book were published, and Walks 3, 7 and 8 partly follow newly signposted 'PR' routes (day walks) with an archaeological theme.

But with the opening of the *Camí* and other trails, perhaps landowners feel justified in deterring visitors from walking anywhere else. Many more locked gates and 'Privado' signs are appearing. Routes off the Camí are already becoming overgrown, and areas where walkers have been permitted for centuries are being closed. All the routes in this book were open to walkers at press date, but the situation can change rapidly, as much to the surprise of Menorcans as to us, judging by locals' forums on the web!

Walk 1: A WALKABOUT TOUR OF MAÓ/MAHON

See town plan on pages 36-37
Distance: 5.7km/3.5mi; 2h10min
Grade: ● easy, but with some steps
Equipment: comfortable shoes of any sort, sunhat, raingear
How to get there and return: 🚌 or 🚐 to/from Maó. There is an underground car park beneath the Plaça de S'Esplanada, but you may find it easier to park beside the harbour road. If you choose the latter, begin and end the walk at the 56min-point.

Shorter walk (2.5km/1.5mi; 1h30min; grade, equipment, access/return as above). Follow the main walk as far as the 16min-point, then turn right and walk beside the Carmen church. Walk in front of the church and cross the Plaça d'Espanya to the far right-hand corner, passing the fish market and the road leading down to the port. Turn right and pick up the main walk again at the 56min-point.

I suppose the people of Menorca and Malta will never agree whether the Grand Harbour at Valletta or Port Maó is the finest harbour in the Mediterranean. That the Royal Navy settled in Valletta in the 19th and 20th centuries was due entirely to the decision of Admiral Lord Nelson. Cynics argue that his choice of Valletta was itself entirely due to the fact that Malta was considerably closer to the court of Naples where Lady Hamilton's husband was British ambassador. For a century before that decision was made, Port Maó had been the home of the British Mediterranean fleet.

The walk begins in the **Plaça de S'Esplanada** (photograph page 39), close to the BUS STATION (**1**). This is the largest and most attractive of a number of squares in Mahón, or Maó as it is usually called now. An 'esplanade' being the space between a citadel and the houses of a town, the name is apt, for on the west side the square is overlooked by BARRACKS (**2**) built during the British occupation. The square was their parade ground. In front of the barracks is the tall **Monument to the Civil War Dead** (**3**).

Stand with your back to the monument and face east. Walk to the street which leads away from the far right hand corner of the square. This is the CARRER DE SES MORERES. Since you will leave this street by turning right, perhaps you should cross over now and walk along the right-hand side.

You can come back on the other side at the end of your tour, but crossing now will give you the opportunity to inspect the bust of Dr Orfila outside no 13, which was his birthplace. Mateu J Orfila (1787-1853) became Professor of Chemistry in the Medical Faculty of the University of Paris, and began the systematic study of poisons. He is regarded as the father of forensic medicine. This street is dedicated to him.

Ignore the street on your right called Cós de Gràcia, and walk the length of Ses Moreres until the crossroads. Here turn right. Maó is built on a not inconsiderable hill above the harbour. The descent is in two stages. This is the first, along CARRER BASTIO and down the COSTA D'EN DEIA. Halfway along, the way bends to the left. Stop here, and look carefully at the building on your left, on the

View across Maó harbour to the naval station and the city's three great churches

ABOUT THE CITY

The harbour at Maó is three and a half miles in length, the longest and deepest of a number of fine harbours on the island. Although the harbourage here is excellent, being bordered by high cliffs it is somewhat inaccessible. However there was one place where a small cove cut into the cliff, and a path ran down to the sea. At the top of the cliff overlooking this cove a fortified village was built in ancient times.

One of the first people on record to have anchored his ships here was a Carthaginian general in 206BC. His name was Mago, brother of Hannibal. When the Romans named the village Municipium Flavianum Magontanum, they may have been naming it after him. Later it was to give its name to mayonnaise!

After the Romans, Vandals and Byzantines in turn occupied Maó until the coming of the Moors, and in 902AD Menorca became part of the Emirate of Cordova. The Moors wanted a harbour nearer to Spain, and built their capital at Ciutadella, but it was here at Maó that the Reconquest of Menorca began.

On 5th January 1287 King Alfonso III of Aragón sailed into the harbour with twenty ships and landed on the Isla del Rei ('the King's Island'). After defeating the Moors, Alfonso resettled the island with Catalans. At various times in the future more and more settlers came from that eastern province of Spain, so that the language of the island came to be a form of Catalan known as 'Menorquín'. (This has been strongly revived since the accession of King Juan Carlos, and most of the former Spanish street names have been replaced with Menorquín names.)

On 1st September 1535 the Turkish naval commander Kheir ed-Din Barbarossa ('Redbeard') sailed under false colours into the harbour, determined to exact vengeance for the sack of Tunis by the Emperor Charles V. The Turkish siege threw up a 'Menorcan Benedict Arnold'. His name was Jaime Scala, the town bailiff. He came to an arrangement with Barbarossa to open the town gates, on the condition that he and his friends were spared. The town was sacked, and Barbarossa sailed away with 800 captives. The following year Jaime Scala was put on trial and executed for treason.

In the next century Maó grew to become the most important town on the island, and the governor Admiral Oquendo moved his residence here. It was during the 18th century that Maó reached its eminence, when Menorca became part of the British Empire. Today, with a population of some 29,000, Maó is the capital of the island and its main shopping centre.

corner — the **Teatro Principal** (**4**). It was built as an opera house in 1829 to the design of an Italian architect. The interior was exquisite. At the bottom of this steep hill is a pretty little square, the **Plaça Reial**, at the heart of a pedestrianised shopping area.

Cross over the square and continue in the same direction along S'ARRAVALETA and into another square, known as the **Plaça del Carmé**. This is dominated by the massive church opposite you, which was built in 1751 as the conventual church of the Carmelite Order of nuns. It is now known as the Carmen or **Carmé Church** (**5**). Baroque in style, its west front is quite plain, although it appears to have once been more ornate. It is worth seeing inside (the side door is in the south wall; you will pass it later in the Shorter walk). When digging the foundations for this church, the workmen unearthed many coins and other objects from the Roman period.

Now that the nuns are no longer here, the cloisters and garden of the convent have been beautifully transformed into a shopping and cultural centre. Cross to the far side of the square and go up steps to enter it. In the basement is a supermarket; small shops and boutiques line the cloisters, and on the first floor are music and art schools. The central garden, **Sa Plaça** (**6**), is now a fine paved square, from where the architecture of the convent buildings can be appreciated.

Leave by the door diagonally opposite the one you came in by. Pass a museum and, at the end of a short street, you will find yourself in the **Plaça Miranda**. Turn left and walk to the end of the square

overlooking the harbour for one of the most beautiful views on the island. Below are the docks; opposite is the naval station.

Now retrace your steps and walk back across the square. Carry straight on to yet another little square — the **Plaça del Príncep** (**16min**). Cross over to the far side, passing an attractive house on your left, and turn left into the CAMÍ D'ES CASTELL. Follow this street to its end, then turn left (referring for a short time to the map on the reverse of the touring map). Pass in front of a petrol station and turn left along Avinguda Fort de l'Eau. At the next roundabout (the one with the anchor) fork right and go down to the HARBOUR (**30min**). Turn left once more to follow the road back into town beside one of the Mediterranean's prettiest harbours. The gloomy island on your right, now an hotel, is the Isla del Rei, and the red-painted house on the headland to the right was once the home of the Commander-in-Chief of the British fleet, Admiral Lord Collingwood.

Approaching the COMMERCIAL DOCK (recognisable by the enormous cruise liner that will almost certainly be moored there), walk a few paces inland to pass the TOURIST INFORMATION OFFICE (**7**) on your right. Then climb the steps on your left up through **Parc Rochina** (**8**). At the top is the **Plaça d'Espanya** (**56min**). Turn right until you are virtually facing the direction you have just come from and, passing the end of the PORTAL DEL MAR, go up the hill beside Parc Rochina into another square. This is the **Plaça de la Conquesta**. On your left is the statue of young Alfonso III himself. He was 18 years old at the

Date palm in Parc Rochina

time of the Reconquest. The statue was given to the city by the late General Franco. The young king's generosity in donating land both to his followers and to the religious orders of St Francis and St Clare earned for him the title 'the Liberal'. (His successor, Jaime II, thought him far too liberal, and reclaimed many of his gifts to the orders.)

The building on the left of the square is **St Mary's Church** (**9**) (Santa María), and facing you is the **Casa Mercadel** (**10**). Once the home of one of Maó's noble families, it was built in 1761 on the foundations of the ancient castle, some of which is incorporated into the interior. This part of the town contains the oldest surviving buildings, and is on the site of the original town, within the medieval walls. The Casa Mercadel is now the Casa de Cultura. It contains a public library, an art gallery, and the town's archives. Turn right in front of the library, and go to the end of CARRER D'ALFONS III, beneath the **Pont d'Es Castell** arch (**11**); here you have another enchanting view of the harbour.

Turn round now, and walk back past the Casa Mercadel and along the narrow cobbled street named after Alfonso III into yet another square, the **Plaça de la Constitució**. On your right is the **Ajuntament** (**12**), the Town Hall. It was first built in 1613, but entirely transformed in 1788. This too is open for inspection. Go up the steps leading from Carrer d'Alfons III to the entrance beneath the clock in the short wall. The clock is English, a gift from the first British lieutenant-governor, Sir Richard Kane. In the

entrance hall are pictures of former governors, the Comte de Lannion and the amiable looking Count of Cifuentes, governor during the period of Spanish rule from 1781 to 1798. There are two inscribed stones of interest. One is the British coat-of-arms that was removed from Fort St Philip when it was destroyed. The other, scarcely decipherable, records the granting of municipal status to the town by the Romans.

At the end of Alfons III turn right, walk past the police station and, at the end, turn left along CARRER D'ISABEL II. This was the street where the medieval royal palace, and later the British governor's palace, were located. Consequently, the Maó aristocracy chose to build its homes here. The present houses date from the 18th century and are in a curious mixture of English and Mediter-ranean styles. The two most apparent debts to English archi-tecture are the sash windows and the absence of balconies. Sash windows are virtually unknown outside the British Isles, except for here in Maó.

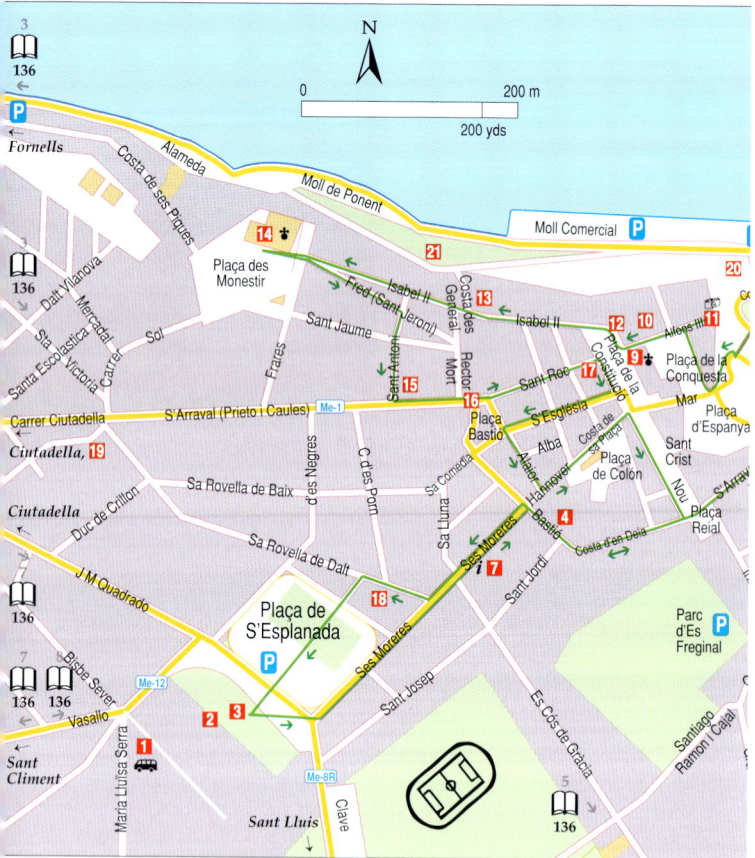

To appreciate these buildings properly you must look upwards. The main state rooms are on the first floor, the *piso principal*, and many still contain fine furniture made by the first-rate Menorcan craftsmen of the 18th century from the pattern books of English cabinet-makers like Chippendale and Sheraton.

Halfway along the street are the **Headquarters of the Military Governor** (**13**). This is where Alfonso III built his palace in the 13th century, and where the British governor built his in the 18th. At first it was of only one storey, and

the style is clearly British colonial. The narrow, arched street beyond it which leads down to the harbour is the COSTA DES GENERAL (or ES PONT des General) and was built either by the Moors, or very soon after the Reconquest.

Having investigated the Costa des General, continue along Isabel II. Notice the plaques above numbers 58, 60 and 62, commemorating illustrious inhabitants who were born or lived there. At the end of Isabel II is the **Plaça des Monestir**, where the **Church of Sant Francesc** (**14**) faces you. Once the friary of the

Maó/Mahón

MAÓ — KEY

1 Bus Station
2 Barracks
3 Monument to the
  Civil War Dead
4 Teatro Principal
5 Carmé (Carmen) Church
6 Sa Plaça
7 Tourist Information (two — one
  at the Port and the other in the
  centre on Ses Moreres)
8 Parc Rochina
9 St Mary's Church (Església Santa
  María)
10 Casa Mercadel (Casa de Cultura)
11 Pont d'Es Castell
12 Ajuntament (Town Hall)
13 Headquarters of the Military
   Governor
14 Church of Sant Francesc
   (St Francis) and Museum of
   Menorcan Antiquities
15 Sala de Cultura (Ermita
   de Sant Antoni)
16 Sant Roc Gate
17 Guard House
18 Science Museum
19 Post Office (off the map, at the
   junction of Carrer Ciutadella
   and J M Quadrado)
20 Customs House
21 Aquarium

Order of St Francis, it is decorated
in a most unusual style, a mixture
of baroque and Romanesque.
Don't be fooled by the doorway —
it was buiIt at the same time as the
rest of the baroque façade
(sometime in the 17th or 18th
centuries). The architect made
similar use of primitive features
inside. You may find it more
difficult to gain admission to this
church than the others in Maó, but
if the opportunity presents itself,
seize it. Then go through the
middle chapel on the right into
one of the most exciting
ecclesiastical experiences in the
town — the Chapel of the
Immaculate Conception.

Spanish religious architecture is
generally almost puritanically
severe — even, as you have already
seen, during the baroque era.
However, there is one exception.
In the 18th century one Spanish
architect went overboard in his
reaction against this tendency. His
name was José Churriguera, and
the style which he invented is
called after him 'churrigueresque'.
Not only did he use baroque
decorative invention to excess, he
crowned it by doing everything in
brilliant white. (Cynics have

dubbed the style, not inappropriately, 'wedding-cake architecture'.) The effect, in small doses, can be stunning, as here. Before leaving, notice the *trompe l'oeil* paintings at the top of the pillars beside the sanctuary.

Next to the church is the **Museum of Menorcan Antiquities** (closed on Mondays in the summer); I heartily recommend a visit — if only to see the cloisters in which it is housed! Leave the museum, cross over the square to return to the town centre along the CARRER FRED (also called Carrer de Sant Jeroni). Take the first turning on the right, which is CARRER DE SANT ANTONI. St Anthony Abad ('Abbot') became the patron saint of Menorca, for it was on his feast day, January 17th, that Alfonso defeated the Moors at Es Vergé. Cross over the Carrer de Sant Jaume and, at the end, you come to S'ARRAVAL (also called Prieto i Caules). On the left, at the corner, is the church *(ermita)* of Sant Antoni, built in classical style. It was restored in 1978 by the Sa Nostra savings bank, and is now the **Sala de Cultura** (**15**), where concerts and exhibitions are held regularly.

Turn left, and there before you is all that remains of the medieval walls, the **Sant Roc Gate** (**16**). Pass through the gate, and walk through the middle of the ancient town along the CARRER DE SANT ROC. This road is the start of the Me-1 which crosses the island to Ciutadella. At the end of Sant Roc you re-enter the **Plaça de la Constitució**.

On your right is the lovely **Guard House** (**17**). Facing you is **St Mary's Church** (**9**). It is the main church of Maó. The present building dates from the middle of the 18th century, but the first church here was begun in 1287, immediately after the Reconquest. Like the Carmen church, its baroque façade is severely plain, but inside it is very different. The magnificent decoration surrounding the main altar and the equally magnificent organ are noteworthy. This splendid instrument was built in Barcelona in 1809 by the Swiss organ builder Kyburz. In the town archives are letters from the bishop to Admiral Lord Collingwood arranging for its transportation and protection at the height of the Napoleonic Wars. It has 4 keyboards, 51 stops and 30,000 pipes. Recitals are given every weekday between 11.00am and 11.30am from June to October on this organ. By the south entrance are two tablets which commemorate the French governors of Menorca, Yacinthe-Cajetan, the Compte de Lannion, and the Marquis de Fremeur.

Turn right at the end of Sant Roc (or cross over the square if you have visited the church) and then turn right again into CARRER DE L'ESGLESIA (Church Street), to walk back up another of the ancient streets to the PLAÇA BASTIO beside the Sant Roc Gate. Turn left at the end, and walk along a delightful little passage, the CARRER D'ALAIOR, into HANNOVER STREET. Named after the British royal family when Menorca was part of the Empire, it is one of the principal shopping streets of Maó. This is quite a steep hill *(costa)*, hence its Menorquín name COSTA DE SA PLAÇA. Turn left and go down the hill, and shortly you pass the square for which the street is named — the **Plaça de Colón**. Having once more arrived at

St Mary's Church, this time turn right along a wide, pedestrianised street, the main shopping street of Maó — CARRER NOU (New Street). Look out for the Casa de Cultura, an exhibition gallery.

At the end, turn right in the **Plaça Reial**, and begin the climb back up COSTA D'EN DEIA and on into CARRER BASTIO. At the junction turn left into Ses Moreres and this time walk on the far side of the street. Cross over Carrer Sa Lluna, but when you come to SA ROVELLADA DE DALT, turn right. You will shortly pass a building with the word 'ATENEU' over the door on your left at number 25. It's the **Science Museum** (18), worth a visit. The intellectual hub of the town, it houses both a library and a natural history museum, as well as providing a meeting-place.

From here, continue along the street and take the first turning to the left, back to the **Plaça de S'Esplanada (2h10min)**.

Plaça de S'Esplanada

Walk 2: THREE WALKS IN S'ALBUFERA DES GRAU NATURAL PARK

Walk a: Cala Sa Torreta (8.5km/ 5.3mi; 2h10min; ● moderate; ascents/descents of only about 80m/260ft, but some rough terrain). Access by 🚌 or 🚗 to/from Es Grau. By car take the Me-7 (Fornells road) from Maó and in 0.75km turn right along the Es Grau road. Park beside the beach (39° 56.931'N, 4° 16.048'E).

Walk b: Zona de Sa Gola (2km/ 1.2mi; 30min; ● very easy, almost level walking). Access as Walk a.

Walk c: Santa Madrona (6km/3.7mi; 1h50min; ● quite easy, with ups and downs of about 150m/500ft). Access by 🚌 only to/from S'Albufera; the road is 2.5km south of Es Grau and signed 'S'Albufera Parc Natural'. Leave your car at the information office/car park (39° 56.380'N, 4° 15.105'E).

Equipment: comfortable shoes, sunhat, raingear, swimwear, picnic, water, suncream, towel, binoculars

These walks are set in the heart of the Albufera Natural Park which actually extends north to Favàritx and Addaia. Walk a — a favourite with readers — visits a magnificent (but seaweedy!) beach backed by a shaded picnic spot … that also happens to be adjacent to a breeding ground for bee-eaters. It used to continue to a talayotic village, which has now been closed off to walkers by the owners of a rural hotel.* Walks b and c take advantage of three trails developed by the island government around the lagoon itself, the largest habitat for water fowl on the island. These walks are shorter than Walk a and, being out-and-back, can be made even shorter — just strolls to the various viewpoints and hides.

Begin Walk a from the BUS STOP/ CAR PARK (**1**) by walking round the large SANDY BEACH of **Es Grau** (Picnic 3) to the cliffs at the far side. You join the CAMÍ DE CAVALLS here: follow the wide path up the cliff and cross the headland. Crossing a saddle, ignore the path which goes off to the right (**2**), and follow the *Camí* to the left as it curves round the end of a small valley. This path keeps turning to the left, passes a couple of paths off to the right, runs through a wall and soon enters a wooded area where you will find an OPEN SHADED SPOT just right for a picnic (another setting for Picnic 3; **20min**). Meeting a junction, keep to the *Camí*, climbing round to the right. Shortly you will reach the top of your climb and come out of the trees to arrive at another junction, where the *Camí* runs downhill to the left (**3**). Ignore it and, keeping ahead, quickly go through a gap in a wall. Ahead you will see Es Grau. Follow the faint path for about 350m, ignoring any turnings to the right, and you will come to another T-junction (**4**). Turn left

---

*Sa Torreta de Tramuntana, the talayotic village, *can* still be visited, but only on Thursdays between 9am and 1pm. Access is via a 5.5km-long cycle track (the Camí de sa Boval) off the Me-7 from Maó to Fornells at KM4.5, on the right. There is no car parking (unless you're staying at the Torre Blanca hotel), so for walkers this would be a *very* long walk.

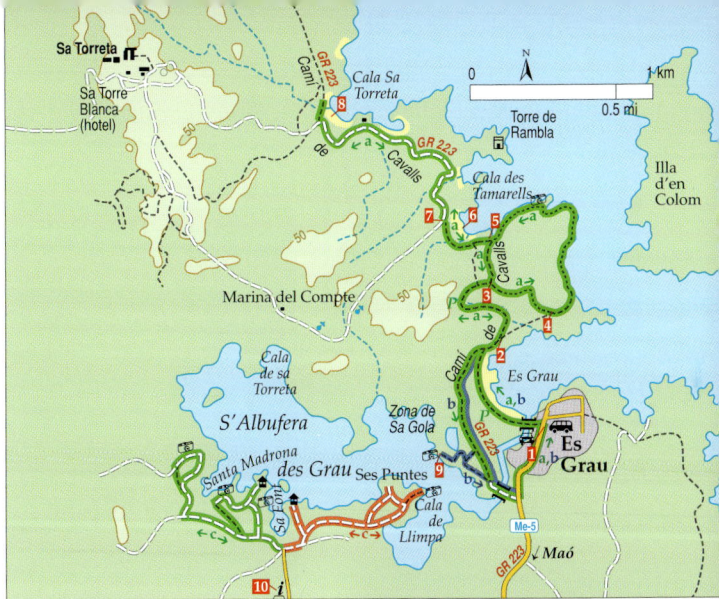

This information board at Es Grau is somewhat deceptive — it only shows the distance out to the viewpoints, not the return. The timings for Walk c are realistic, but allow 30 minutes for the visit to La Gola.

here on a clearer path and head in the direction of the island known as Illa d'en Colom.

When you reach the cliffs, follow the path down to your left and walk along the edge of the cliffs. Eventually the path will fork, only to rebraid itself further on. Soon you will see below you an exquisite tiny beach, and at the end of the headland you will have a good view of an old watchtower and the lighthouse at Favàritx. Users say that this part of the walk, on the headland, despite the rather rough terrain, compensates for the loss of the talayotic village, and that it is quite easy to get down to the 'exquisite sandy beach'.

Carry on round the edge of the cliff until, at the far side, you find yourself back on the *Camí* (**5**), a clearly discernible path. Follow the path down to sea level again and round the bay, past two small inlets

and a sandy beach (**Cala des Tamarells**; **6**), then up the slope on the far side. A tiny sandy path takes you through a gap in a wall and down to the left, where you join a TRACK (**7**; **50min**).

Turn right and follow the track northwest, past a northerly **Cala des Tamarells** — towards the Torre de Rambla and into a new, pretty valley. After a couple of ups

MENORCAN GATES

Look out for the aesthetically pleasing gates that still frequently stand at the entrance to farms and fields (the one in the photograph on page 88 is a good example). Made to a traditional Menorcan design from the twisted wood of wild olive trees, once they were universal, but lately farmers have been replacing them with sturdier iron ones like the one shown above — far less pleasing to the eye.

Gates have attracted more correspondence from 'Landscapers' who use this book than any other subject. Let me try to clarify the matter. There are many references to gates and gateways in these walks, even across some minor public roads. They are mostly there to prevent cattle from straying. Farmers cannot afford to take the chance that people using the roads can be relied upon to close the gates securely behind them, so they will often padlock them (although not usually on public roads). So, depending on whether there is livestock in the vicinity, a gate may be open or closed. If the latter, it may be latched, secured with twine or

Top left: iron gate with a charming notice for walkers (seen many years ago on Walk 9). Above: S'Albufera, a salt-water lagoon, is at the heart of Menorca's Biosphere Reserve (top); Cala des Tamarells with its pretty coves and watchtower, the Torre de Rambla

padlocked. Hence you may be able to walk through the gate, need to open and secure it behind you, or climb over an adjacent wall. Where you are meant to climb over a wall, there will usually be **protruding stones** *(botadores)* to help you over the hurdle.

Where there are no gaps in the wall nor 'stepping stones', there will usually be an accompanying 'Privado' notice, and I would urge you to respect that — despite the clear GPS tracks you may have seen posted by walkers on the web!

and downs, the *Camí* runs past a tiny isolated white house and along the back of **Cala Sa Torreta** (or Cala Rambles; **8**; **45min**), a very beautiful and almost always deserted beach. Deserted, because it is probably the most seaweedy beach in Menorca. To your left

pine trees provide the shaded picnic spot shown opposite. The small holes you may see in the sand bank are the nesting places of bee-eaters. If you are not an ornithologist, look for something a bit smaller than a pigeon and as colourful as a parrot.

Cala Sa Torreta is a pleasant place to picnic — nearby is a breeding ground for bee-eaters

Now, since it's no longer possible to go on to Sa Torreta, retrace the Camí de Cavalls back to **Es Grau (2h10min)**.

Start Walk b (the Park's blue trail) by following WALK A to the CAMÍ DE CAVALLS, where you turn left through a gap in the sand dunes and head along the sandy track through woodland. This is the **Zona de Sa Gola**, a 'Region of Special Natural Interest'. In a few minutes, at a 'MIRADOR' sign, follow an impressive path on raised decking across a field towards **S'Albufera**. It takes you up a small hill to a platform, for a superb VIEW (**9**) of the lagoon.

On your return from the viewpoint, turn right where the decking forks. When you reach the main path/*Camí*, bear right. A track takes you across a footbridge and to the tarmac road. Turn left, back to the car park/bus stop at **Es Grau (30min)**.

My **Walk c** combines the Park's GREEN (3KM) AND RED (2KM) TRAILS, making a fairly satisfying series of loops lasting an hour and 50 minutes — or much longer if you're bird-watching. It doesn't matter in which order you walk the trails. Both have ample signposting and information boards about flora, fauna and Menorca's environmental and cultural heritage. There are charming hides at the start of each trail, meaning that birdwatchers need not do the entire route.

Do be sure to call in at the **Centre de Interpretació** to learn more about the Biosphere Reserve. (The whole island was declared a World Biosphere Reserve by UNESCO in 1993, and S'Albufera is at its heart, covering a total area of over 5000 hectares supporting vastly diverse habitats.)

Then **start the walk** from the INFORMATION CENTRE CAR PARK (**10**): walk north for 450m to a turning circle where the signposted trails begin.

Walk 3: ES VERGE AND THE ERMITA DE SANT JOAN

See map on reverse of touring map; see also photos on pages 33, 35, 39

Distance: 11km/6.8mi; 2h25min

Grade: ● easy, on metalled lanes; overall ascent/descent 100m/330ft

Equipment: comfortable foot-wear, sunhat, suncream, raingear, picnic

How to get there and return: As Walk 1, page 32, but by 🚌 park

either at the Plaça de S'Esplanada or at the western end of the harbour (the 15min-point in the main walk).

Shorter walk: Ermita de Sant Joan (4km/2.5mi; 1h10min; grade, equipment, access as above). Follow the main walk to the 40min-point at **4**, then skip to the 1h55min-point to end this stroll.

T his short and delightful walk is steeped in history. It takes you first along part of the Maó waterfront and then through the fertile market gardens of Es Vergé, to the little Ermita de Sant Joan. From here you follow Kane's Dyke. Returning to the *ermita*, you make your way back to Maó along a narrow lane of considerable antiquity, with splendid views over the plain.

Start out in **Maó** by standing with your back towards the **Monument to the Civil War Dead** in the **Plaça de S'Esplanada** (**1**; see the town plan on pages 36-37). Leave the square by the far left-hand corner and turn left into CARRER DE SA ROVELLADA DE DALT. Follow it round until you reach S'ARRAVAL. Cross over and continue ahead along CARRER DEL SOL, descending until you are in sight of St Francis' church and the Museum of Menorcan Antiquities. Bear left now and follow COSTA DE SES PIQUES downhill. Halfway down, turn right and go down STEPS TO THE PORT (**2**). The monument on your left was raised in 1785 by the people of Mahon in gratitude to the Count of Cifuentes (see page 37). Turn left and follow the road to the end of the harbour (**15min**).

Take the road on the left sign-posted 'FORNELLS', not the one which goes across the end of the harbour. This is quite a busy road, and you should walk on the left-hand side of it. However, you will

not be on it for long. It is the start of the main road which the first British lieutenant-governor of the island, Sir Richard Kane, had built to link Ciutadella with Maó in the 18th century (the Menorcans know it as the 'CAMI D'EN KANE'). It runs parallel with the modern road (Me-1), about a kilometre to the north, as far as Es Mercadal, from where the Me-1 follows the line of Kane's road for the rest of the way. Before the British occupation, travel had been along the 'Old Road', the Camí Vell, first built by the Romans. It is significant that whereas the modern road goes to Maó town, Kane built his road straight to the harbour. That was the only interest Britain had in Menorca: a base for its Mediterranean fleet. Inciden-tally, Kane arranged for his road to be paid for in a very English way. He put a tax on alcohol.

In 200 metres/yards you come to a ROUNDABOUT. Turn left and walk up the hill for 60m/yds, then cross the ring road *carefully*. On the far side, walk ahead on asphalt for

On the Camí de Baix de Sant Joan (left) and the Ermita de Sant Joan

40m/yds to a T-junction. Turn left here on a country lane, the Camí de Baix de Sant Joan (**3**; **30min**). You make your way through **Es Vergé**, between some of the most important market gardens on Menorca, which provide Maó with its salad crops and vegetables. It is very peaceful down here, and the world of the tourist resorts seems far away indeed. It was here, at the head of the harbour, that eighteen year old Alfonso III met and defeated the Moorish army on 17th January 1287 and regained Menorca for Christendom. If you look over to your right, on the far side of the Fornells road, you will see a memorial which the people of Menorca raised to Sir Richard Kane in 1924.

After 650m/0.4mi the lane passes a little church on the left, the **Ermita de Sant Joan** (St John the Baptist; **4**; **40min**). This was clearly a place of communal importance in bygone days, with its stone seats around the little square. It had a neglected air when I first visited, but it has been wonderfully refreshed during the pandemic,

and it makes a wonderful place for a quiet picnic (Picnic 1). One of the island's first day-walk trails comes in here, the PR Me 1 from Dalt de Sant Joan to Alcaidús.

From the chapel follow the road as it bends to the right and right again. *(But for the Shorter walk, skip to the 1h55min-point below.)* After 500m/0.4mi you cross a bridge and come to a T-junction. To continue the walk you will turn left, but before doing so you may wish to make a short detour to visit the **Kane Memorial** (**5**) which you can see a short distance to the right along the Fornells road. For the rest of the outward part of the walk your way is beside a drainage ditch. Until the 18th century much of this plain was marshland. In order to build his new road across it, Kane had this ditch dug to drain the marsh, transforming it into rich agricultural land. The ditch abounds with vegetation and birds; keep beside it, ignoring all turns on the right to farmhouses. Eventually you CROSS THE DITCH (**6**), and the road reverts to track.

Where the track divides, fork right (**7**; **1h**) along the CAMI D'ATZAGODARS and follow a walled-in track past bamboo. After heavy rain the track may be too muddy, forcing you to turn round here to continue the walk from the 1h25min-point, but most of the time you should be able to continue. You pass a pretty WHITE FARMHOUSE and carry on along a narrow metalled lane beside the dyke as far as a T-junction, where you turn left. Keep walking for a few more minutes, until PRIVATE PROPERTY (**8**) blocks your way.

Turn back here, enjoy the view, and retrace your steps past the white farm down to the MEADOW (**1h25min**). Turn left and walk along the path by a high wall. Make your way back to the T-junction and turn right over the bridge, continuing as far as the **Ermita de Sant Joan** (**4**; **1h55min**). Turn right and walk in front of the church and between the trees. Take the CAMI DE DALT DE SANT JOAN (**9**; also the PR Me 1) on your left; it climbs the hill behind a house. This is an ancient cart-road, which in the days before Kane drained the marsh was the only way from the farms of Es Vergé into Maó. Deep ruts made by cartwheels in the bedrock proclaim how much use this road has seen.

Soon you will come to where the modern harbour road (the RM dual carriageway ring road) cuts across the ancient one. Cross over with care and patience and go up a narrow path opposite. When the path turns right you will see that you are back on the ancient road. Most of the paving consists of small uneven cobbles, which was the normal Menorcan way of surfacing roads. Very occasionally, as in one section here (just before

the track reaches the outskirts of the town), the paving is much more sophisticated and gives a clue to the origin of the road. Only the Romans surfaced roads with that much care before the 20th century, on Menorca or anywhere else (see panel on page 63).

The old road ends beside an INFANTS' SCHOOL (**2h10min**). Keep straight ahead, still on the CAMÍ DE DALT DE SANT JOAN, and cross over Carrer Cronista Riudavets. Continue in the same direction along CARRER SANTA VICTORIA, crossing **Plaça D'Eivissa**, Dalt Vilanova and Santa Escolàstica; then come to a T-junction with CARRER SOL. Referring once more to the town plan on pages 36-37, turn right and follow this street to its junction with S'Arraval. Now, if you are in a hurry, cross over and follow Sa Rovellada de Dalt; in just over 200m/yds, it will bring you back to the Esplanade Square.

Otherwise one more pleasure awaits you, especially if it is early evening. Turn left, and go along S'ARRAVAL as far as the **Sant Roc Gate**. Pass through the gate, go down the hill, cross the **Plaça de la Constitució**, and make your way along the narrow cobbled CARRER D'ALFONS III between the Ajuntament (Town Hall) and St Mary's Church. Cross the **Plaça de la Conquesta** and go on beneath the arch of the **Pont d'Es Castell**, to the VIEWPOINT over Parc Rochina and the harbour. Then walk back along ALFONS III to the **Plaça de la Constitució**, turn left and cross the square diagonally, to go up the hill of COSTA DE SA PLAÇA (Hannover) on the far left. Walk into SES MORERES and back to the **Plaça de S'Esplanada** (**2h25min**).

Walk 4: FORT ST PHILIP AND MAHON HARBOUR

See map on reverse of touring map; see also photos on pages **33, 35, 39, 54, 56 and 57**
Distance: 16km/10mi; 4h
Grade: ● easy, with overall ascents/descents of about 150m/490ft; a few rough paths
Equipment: comfortable but sturdy footwear, sunhat, raingear, suncream, picnic (or have lunch in one of the restaurants en route), plenty of water
How to get there and return:
🚌 or 🚐 to/from Maó. By car, park in the car park beneath Esplanade Square. Alternatively take the ring road round Maó, following signs for Es Castell. Park at the far side of the town, by the roundabout west of Cala Figuera (39° 53.035'N, 4° 16.290'E), and begin the walk at the 25min-point. At the end, turn to the start of the walk and follow the directions for the first 25 minutes to get back to your car.

Shorter or Alternative walks

1 Maó and harbour (4.5km/2.8mi; 1h; grade, equipment, access/return as above). Follow the walk for 28min to **2**, then turn left and walk Costa de Cala Figuera past the car park to the harbour road. Turn left and pick up the walk again, shortly after the 3h15min-point at **10**.

2 Countryside and Fort St Philip (12.3km/7.6mi; 3h; grade, equipment as main walk); access: 🚌 to Maó, then 🚌 to Es Castell, or 🚐 to Es Castell; park by the Military Museum (39° 52.777'N, 4° 17.416'E). Pick up the main walk at **9** (the Military Museum). Shortly after the 3h15min-point, at Cala Figuera (**2**), go up Costa Cala Figuera at the right of the car park and turn left to climb to the top of the hill. Cross the road, then follow the walk from the 28min-point back to the 2h55min-point at **9**. Return by 🚌 from Es Castell to Maó, then 🚌 from Maó, or 🚐 from Es Castell.

3 Maó harbour (4.5km/2.8mi; 1h05min; grade, equipment as main walk; access: 🚌 or 🚐 to Maó, then 🚌 to Es Castell). Begin the walk at **9** (the Military Museum) and follow it to the end.

4 Maó, countryside and Fort St Philip (11.3km/7mi; 2h55min; grade, equipment as above; access: 🚌 or 🚐 to Maó). Follow the main walk to the 2h55min-point at **9**. Turn left along Carrer de Victori, and you will soon see the bus stop on your left, near the roundabout. Return by 🚌 from Es Castell to Maó, then 🚌 or 🚐 from Maó.

This is perhaps the most interesting walk on the island. The outward part takes you through 18th-century Maó, on through farming country, and then beside the coast, to bring you to the scant remains of what was once one of the Mediterranean's greatest fortresses: Fort St Philip. You return beside one of its longest and most beautiful harbours.

Start out in **Maó** by standing with your back towards the **Monument to the Civil War Dead** in the **Plaça de S'Esplanada** (**1**; see town plan on pages 36-37). Leave the square by heading east along CARRER DE SES MORERES in the far right-hand corner. Turn right at the end along CARRER DE BASTIO, then walk down the hill of COSTA D'EN DEIA. Continue across the **Plaça Reial** into S'ARRAVALETA. Walk along the right-hand side of the **Plaça del Carmé** into the

Plaça del Príncep. Take the right-hand road at the fork ahead, and make your way along the CAMI D'ES CASTELL. The *castell* was the great 16th-century fortress of St Philip, which guarded the entrance to Maó harbour. After passing the Andrea Doria flats at the end of the town, you will come to a large ROUNDABOUT (**25min**). Keep straight on, across the roundabout.

On your left is an arm of the harbour now known as **Cala Figuera** (**2**; **28min**). In former times the *cala* was called the 'English Creek', for a freshwater stream ran into the sea here, and ships of the Royal Navy would put in to take on water. Formerly, petrol was stored in the area; now it is a car park. *(Shorter walk 1 leaves here.)* Almost opposite the *cala*, a road (the CAMI D'EN VERD) goes off to the right. *(Shorter walk 2 joins here.)* Follow this road for 50m/yds, looking for a narrow walled-in footpath on the left. Go along the footpath, then up steps to join the CAMI DE BINIATAP. Turn left. After a few metres, ignore a track on the left, and follow your road round to the right. In four minutes ignore Carrer Tropical on the left leading to the houses of **Son Vilar**. As you walk along the Camí de Biniatap look out on your left for a large defensive tower adjacent to an old farmhouse (see panel on page 125). Ignore another road on the left, and two minutes later cross straight over the road which runs from Trepucó to Es Castell. Continue along a tarmac road past the Es Castell industrial estate *(Polígon industrial)*.

Some 10m after passing Carrer d'es Fusters on the left, at a Y-fork (**3**; **50min**), go right. After 50m

turn left along a walled-in lane — still the Camí de Biniatap. The lane loses its asphalt surface but continues, metalled, past the Camí de Rafal on the left and a narrow cycle track on the right. Running between stone walls and past various *fincas,* the Camí de Biniatap continues all the way to the SANT LLUIS/ES CASTELL ROAD (Me-6).

Cross over towards a white farmhouse (the front of which is shown on page 51) and follow the track to its left. In three minutes bear right (going straight ahead) when you reach a tarmac road. As you walk along this road you have a fine view of the military base of Sa Mola to your left. In six minutes ignore a lane on your left, and shortly pass the farm of SES AUBERTONAS. Next door is the MILITARY AREA WITH THE AERIAL MASTS you may have noticed earlier (**4**). After you have passed the entrance to the base and the farm of Sant Joan de Binissaida, turn left on a wide dirt road (the CAMI DE SA TORRA) signposted 'HORTS DE BINISSAIDA'. Here look to your right, where between the trees you may be able to spot the sturdy tower of the old FORTIFIED FARMHOUSE shown on page 57 (**1h26min**).

Follow this road for 600m/ 0.35mi, ignoring all side tracks, until you arrive in front of the large wooden gates of the Villa Eugenia. Turn left into a narrow walled-in track called CAMI DE SA CALA, briefly joining the CAMI DE CAVALLS. Where the grounds of the villa finish, turn right and leave the track by climbing through a gap in the wall. Follow a well-walked path across fields and through more gaps in walls towards the sea, arriving just to the

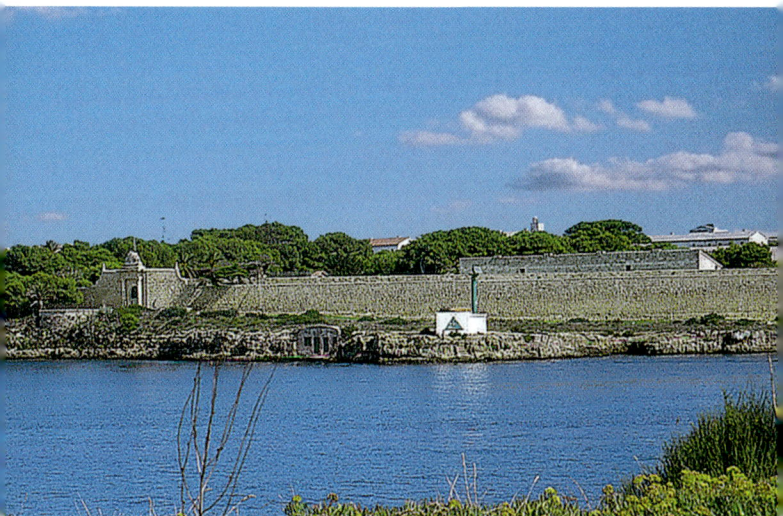

Maó harbour, with the 18th-century quarantine hospital on Lazareto Island. It was hoped the high walls would prevent plague from reaching the city.

left of a defensive tower built during the Napoleonic War, the **Torre d'en Penjat** (**5**).

Turn left and walk beside the sea (Picnic 2) for 10 minutes, until you reach another, older tower. To the right you can see where stone has been quarried to build these fortifications. Since everything on the island has been built of stone from time immemorial, you will frequently come across old quarries when walking. Picnic 10 is set in one near Alaior, and near Ciutadella some have been developed as tourist attractions (see Walk 21).

Make your way round or over the tower, and join a tarmac road which turns left to follow the edge of the beautiful **Cala de Sant Esteve**, known for a hundred years to British servicemen as St Stephen's Creek. Over the creek you can see all that remains of Fort St Philip. After Barbarossa had destroyed Maó in 1535, the

Emperor Charles V gave orders that a fort should be built on the south side of the harbour mouth. The work, entrusted to an Italian engineer named Juan Bautista Calvi, began in 1554. During the 18th century the British spent £1.5 million on strengthening its defences. However, during the Spanish occupation of the island from 1781-98, King Carlos III gave orders for its demolition; a curious act of unilateral disarmament which enabled General Sir Charles Stuart to retake the island without the loss of a single British life when the outbreak of the Napoleonic Wars made a Mediterranean base for the Royal Navy once again imperative.

On your left you will see the entrance to a small fort built to provide crossfire with Fort St Philip. Named after a great British general, it was known as the **Marlborough Redoubt** (**6**). In the final assault in 1781, a captain and 50 men withstood a French force of 700 men. It is said to be connected to Fort St Philip by a subterranean passage beneath the *cala*. The redoubt may be visited for a small fee (it is usually closed during the early afternoon). When you have explored the redoubt, continue round the *cala* as it bends to the right. When you have finally walked round the end of it, look carefully for a NARROW FOOTPATH (**7**) on your left by a clump of bamboo and climb it. This path (part of the Camí de Cavalls) is in fact one of the oldest roads on the island, built by the Romans; originally it continued to Maó.

At the top of the path, stop and turn round before continuing your walk. From here you have a splendid view of the redoubt. Now bear left, ignore a track on your left, and walk to the junction with the Cf-2. Turn left again, and in four minutes you will come to a crossroads beside a CEMETERY (**2h17min**). Turn right now along the AVINGUDA DEL PORT into **Sol del Este**. Ignoring three roads on the left, follow the PASSEIG MARÍTIM round to the left until you come to the CAFETERIA SOL DEL ESTE. The walk continues to the left from here, but for an interesting detour, turn right and walk towards the sea on Passeig de sa Font Dolça, then turn right again until you come to a wall with stile which will give you access to the SITE OF **Fort St Philip** (**8**). (You may explore as far as the barbed wire fence, but beyond, as you will see, the *zona militar* is still occupied by the Spanish Regiment of Artillery.) This is the setting for Picnic 17, a superb spot where you can watch the cruise liners entering and leaving the harbour.

Across the water can be seen

the fortifications built on Sa Mola in the 1840s to replace Fort St Philip in giving protection to the harbour mouth. They were never finished. The large island in front of it is known as Illa del Llatzeret (Lazareto) and was used to house victims of the plague. The high walls, it was hoped, would prevent infection being blown into Maó.

Retrace your steps to the end of the *passeig* beside the Cafetería Sol del Este and carry on along the Passeig Marítim, rounding the headland and turning into **Cala Padera**. At the T-junction with CARRER D'ES POUET, turn right, cross the plaza and walk up steps. On joining CARRER XALOC, turn right. This takes you into CARRER GREGAL, where you turn left.

At the end of Carrer Gregal, at a car parking area, turn right to some steps. Go down these to the edge of the water and turn left. Walk along the wooden mooring platform for a few metres/yards, into **Cala Fonts**, the harbour of **Es Castell**. The name of the town has changed over the centuries. Having grown up as a settlement nestling in the shadow of Fort St Philip, it was first known as Philipstown. When the French attacked the fort in 1756, its houses gave them excellent cover. After the island was returned to Britain, orders were given for Philipstown to be demolished and a new town built further away. It was named Georgetown, in honour of King George III. Like Maó, its architecture is similar to 18th-century English buildings. When Menorca reverted to Spain, the town was renamed Villa Real de San Carlos, in honour of one of the most enlightened monarchs of the century, Carlos III. Its name was shortened to Villa-Carlos, but it is always referred to locally as Es Castell, on account of its proximity to Es Castell de Sant Felip — Fort St Philip.

Walk up the hill on the left of the harbour and keep straight ahead on the main street, CARRER STUART (named after General Stuart). Walk across the **Plaça de S'Esplanada** — once the parade ground of the British soldiery whose old barracks surround the square. Now one has been turned into housing, while the **Cuartel de Cala Corp** (**9**; **2h55min**) is the military museum. *(Shorter walks 2 and 3 begin here; Shorter walk 4 ends here.)* Continuing along Carrer Stuart, you pass the street leading to the smaller harbour, Cala Corb. Carrer Stuart ends at the junction with Carrer Fontanilles. Cross over and bear diagonally right into CARRER AGAMENON. Follow Carrer Agamenón past the eponymous hotel as far as a turning circle beside a yellow house. Turn left along an unmade road and 10m/yds further on bear right on a narrow path. Where the path divides twice, choose the right hand fork each time, so that you head for the cliff edge and follow the path across a field, beside the harbour. Ahead, the lovely red building is the Hotel del Almirante, named after the admiral Lord Collingwood, commander-in-chief of the Mediterranean fleet, who lived here during the Napoleonic Wars. In seven minutes, when the path divides, keep right, descending to pass in front of some white houses. This sometimes-overgrown path may be difficult to spot at first, but it quickly leads to a concrete path and then steps down to the HARBOUR ROAD (**10**; **3h15min**).

Turn left and follow this road

Farm near the Sant Lluís/Es Castell road

round **Cala Figuera** (**2**). *(Shorter walk 1 rejoins here; Shorter walk 2 climbs up past the car parking area.)* Continuing beside **Maó harbour**, after half an hour you will be at the COMMERCIAL DOCK. Again referring to the town plan, climb steps on the left up through **Parc Rochina**. Turn right at the top, up CARRER SANT CRIST, then go left into CARRER NOU. At the end you return to the **Plaça Reial**. Turn right and climb back up COSTA D'EN DEIA, turning left at the crossroads to follow SES MORERES back to the **Plaça de S'Esplanada** (**4h**).

Walk 5: TREPUCO

See map on reverse of touring map; see also photo on page 39 and drawings on pages 12-13
Distance: 5.3km/3.3mi; 1h15min
Grade: easy, almost level walking

Equipment: comfortable shoes of any sort, sunhat, raingear, suncream
How to get there and return: as Walk 1, page 32

The prehistoric settlement at Trepucó has a double advantage: it's near to Maó and has the largest monuments on Menorca. The original excavation of the site was undertaken in 1931 by Dr Margaret Murray and a team from Cambridge University.

Start out in **Maó** by standing with your back towards the **Monument to the Civil War Dead** in the **Plaça de S'Esplanada** (**1**; see town plan on pages 36-37). Leave the square by heading east along CARRER DE SES MORERES in the right-hand corner. Then take the first turning on the right, Es Cos DE GRACIA. In 300m/yds you cross Carrer Santiago Ramon i Cajal and, after another 200m/yds, pass two more roads on your left. Now referring to the back of the touring map, bear slightly right, to the ROUNDABOUT (**2**). Cross over the busy dual carriageway and keep straight ahead on a country lane (Me-4) with a magenta sign for 'POBLAT DE TREPUCO', soon passing the CEMETERY on the left. Ignore Camí d'en Barrotes on the right, a road on the left, and in a while Camí de Binitalfa straight ahead. Follow your road round to the left, and soon you will arrive at more crossroads. Turn right to the site of **Trepucó** (**3**; **27min**).

TREPUCO

The monuments of Trepucó were built during the second millennium BC, at about the time Moses was leading the children of Israel out of Egypt. The first people to see them in modern times believed that only giants could have lifted the huge stones and attributed them to Homer's Cyclops, hence the term 'cyclopean' which is sometimes used as an alternative to 'megalithic' (Greek for 'big stones') to describe this kind of architecture.

In this photo, the *taula* (the largest on Menorca) rises in front of the massive *talayot*. In the adjacent field to the west, part of the village has been excavated (see illustration on page 13), revealing amongst much else a 'hypostyle chamber', with typical pillar and one roofing slab still in place.

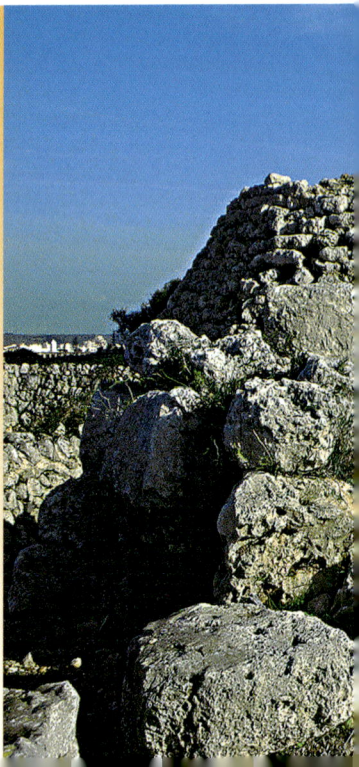

Twice during the 18th century Britain briefly lost control of Menorca to the French — in 1756 (to the Duc de Richelieu) and in 1782 (to the Duc de Crillon, at the head of a joint French and Spanish army). While he was besieging Fort St Philip, the Duc de Crillon mounted his artillery on the *talayot* of Trepucó and built the thick defensive wall which still surrounds the site, using stones from nearby *talayots*. Yet it is the gigantic *taula* which has pride of place here. The stone circle surrounding it led the first English historian of Menorca, John Armstrong, to conclude (erroneously) that it was the work of Druids. It is the largest on the island. You can find out more about these monuments on pages 12-13.

When you leave the site, turn left and, on reaching the crossroads, take the road opposite (signposted 'CAMI D'EN VERD') and bear right. This pleasant country lane is some 1.3km/0.8mi long and will bring you to the Maó/Es Castell road at Cala Figuera. En route, in about ten minutes, you will be able to look along the road and across the harbour directly at a lovely red house proudly standing on top of the far cliff. It is Golden Farm, linked in legend with Admiral Lord Nelson.

Just before the end of the Camí d'en Verd you pass a CAVE on your right. The lane passes next through what was once a QUARRY and brings you to a T-junction with the MAHON/ES CASTELL ROAD (**4**; **50min**). Turn left here. You now have a choice of ways. Either follow the directions below, which take you through the town, or, if you prefer to walk beside the harbour, descend Costa Cala Figuera after a few paces and pick

up Walk 4 shortly after its 3h15min-point at **2** (page 51).

To walk through the town, go up the hill to Maó on the Me-2. Keep straight ahead at the ROUND-ABOUT, between a petrol station and the Andrea Doria flats. Continue along CAMI D'ES CASTELL for 200m/yds, and turn left on CARRER DE SANT MANUEL at the crossroads. Then take the third turning on the right, CARRER DE LA INFANTA. Follow it past three streets on the left. You come to CARRER DE GRACIA (if necessary, refer again to the town plan on pages 36-37). Turn left along Carrer de Gràcia, but in a few metres/yards keep right along CARRER SANTIAGO RAMON I CAJAL, passing the **Parc d'Es Freginal** (**1h10min**) on the right. At the next junction, turn right and follow ES COS DE GRACIA back to its junction with CARRER DE SES MORERES. Turn left to the **Plaça de S'Esplanada** (**1h15min**).

Golden Farm, seen from the distance on Walks 4, 5 and 6: it is thought that Admiral Lord Nelson stayed here for five days in 1799, and popular legend has it that Lady Hamilton accompanied him.

WALK 6: ST STEPHEN'S CREEK AND BINISSAIDA

See map on reverse of the touring map; see also photos on pages 49 and opposite
Distance: 9.8km/6mi; 2h15min
Grade: easy, almost level walking on lanes and some stony paths
Equipment: comfortable but sturdy footwear, sunhat, suncream, long trousers, long sleeves, rainwear, picnic (or have lunch in one of the restaurants in Sol del Este or Es Castell), plenty of water
How to get there and return: 🚌 to/from Es Castell (you will probably have to get a bus to Maó first) or 🚗 to Es Castell. There is a large car park beside the Me-2 close to the bus stop and football ground (39° 52.610'N, 4° 17.372'E).

H ere is a most enjoyable walk along the beautiful coast just south of the entrance to Maó harbour, in a region filled with historical associations. Since it partly overlaps with Walk 4, additional information can be found on pages 47-51.

Start out at the ROUNDABOUT (**1**) by the BUS STOP and CAR PARK in **Es Castell** on the main MAHON/ ES CASTELL Road (Me-2). Head southeast on the Me-2 for just under 1km, until you come to a crossroads. Keep straight ahead here and pass a CEMETERY on the left (**12min**).

If after very heavy rain the depression in the road just past the cemetery is flooded, you will be grateful for the raised causeway at the side, as doubtless the Redcoats would have been on their way to Fort St Philip which lay at the end of this road, where the military area is now. Turn right at the next JUNCTION (**2**) and in six minutes, at the top of a hill, ignore a track to the right and look ahead. Furthest away, on top of the cliff, is the Torre d'en Penjat, a watch-tower built during the Napoleonic War, and before it and to its left is the Marlborough Redoubt, built to provide crossfire with Fort St Philip. Some 60m/yds further on, fork right down a signposted path beneath power lines. Lower down, notice its extraordinarily fine cobbled surface, which in all likelihood was laid as long ago as the time of the Roman occupation of Menorca (see panel on page 63). At the bottom (**7**), turn right and walk round **Cala de Sant Esteve** (St Stephen's Creek), past the entrance to the **Marlborough Redoubt** (**6**; **26min**).

At the end of the creek follow the road uphill to where, at the end of a small PARKING AREA (**3**), a path to the left goes through bushes, to steps which take you to the top of a little tower. But *take care,* because there is a large hole where once the roof was. Keep climbing and follow a narrow path in the direction of the **Torre d'en Penjat** (**5**). As you do so, notice on your left how the cliff has been quarried away to provide stone to build the fort. Turn to page 77 to read of the unfortunate experience of Admiral Byng in these waters.

At the end of a solid wall going down from the Torre d'en Penjat to the water's edge (**45min**), you may find a GAP where you can go down steps and follow the coast south for a some distance, walking between the sea on your left and a wall on your right. But since the opening of the Camí de Cavalls, the path has become blocked by mastic bushes.

The main walk, however, turns

right here. Walk past the tower and across the thistly fields for 200m, to where a gap in a facing wall gives access to a walled-in path, the CAMÍ DE SA CALA (**4**; also the CAMÍ DE CAVALLS). Turn left and walk between the walls. This path — an ancient donkey trail — in common with many others on the island which run between drystone walls, was in constant danger of being blocked by intrusive mastic bushes. Thanks to ongoing maintenance of the Camí de Cavalls, it is easy going now — which was not the case when this book was first written!

Emerging briefly by the GATES OF VILLA EUGENIA (**5**), the *Camí* then runs back between stone walls

MENORCA

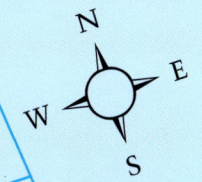

KEY/LEGENDE

0 ———— 5 km / 3 mi

	dual carriageway/Schnellstraße
	main road/Hauptstraße
	secondary road/Nebenstraße
	motorable track/Fahrweg
	0-100 m (0-325 ft)
	100-200 m (325-655 ft)
	200-300 m (655-985 ft)
	over/über 300 m (985 ft)

🚗2 area of the car tour and number/Gebiet der Autotour mit zugehöriger Nummer

8 area of the walk and number Gebiet der Wanderung mit zugehöriger Nummer

route of Camí de Cavalls and starting points/Verlauf des Camí de Cavalls und Startpunkte

🏨🍴 Hotel.Restaurant
⛽ petrol station/Tankstelle
⛪ church.chapel/Kirche.Kapelle
★ tourist attraction/Sehenswürdigkeit
🏰 fort.watchtower/Festung.Wachtturm
🏛 site/prähistorische Siedlung
⊕ medical centre/Krankenhaus
🪑 picnic tables/Picknicktische
📷 viewpoint/Aussichtspunkt

Alaior

71

Sa Carretera

Ciutadella

Me-1

Fornells

Es Grau

N

0   1 km
0.5 mi

Camí d'en Kane

150

Camí d'en Kane

Me-7

Me-5

GR 223

Cala Mesquida

Cala de Cavalls

Sa Mesquida

Es Murtar

La Argentina

La Argentina

Camí de Cavalls

Sant Antoni
(Golden Farm)

GR 223

Me-3

Torralba
Torralba d'en Salort
Torralba Vell

Sant Rafael

Rafal Rubí

PR Me 1

Santa Elisabet

Alcaidús de Dalt

PR Me 1

Kane Memorial

GR 223

Camí de Cavalls

Estación Naval

Mahón/Maó

36-37

Camí de Cavalls

Cala Llonga

Illa del Rei

Illa Plana

PR Me 1

Ermita de Sant Joan

Es Vergé

Me-1

Central

Cala Figuera

Illa del Llatzeret

Sa Mola

Me-1

Talatí de Dalt

Camí Vell d'Alaior

Algendar de Sa Costa

PR Me 1

Polígon industrial

Ronda

Cala Corb

Illa del Rei

Es Castell

Cala Fonts

Son Vilar

Cala Padera

Me-4

Me-2

GR 223

10

Torrellisa Vell

Camí de Mussulá

Basílica des Fornàs de Torelló

Curnia Vey
Curnia Nou

Sa Cudia

Barrotes

Trepucó

Camí d'en Verd

Polígon industrial

Sol del Este

Es Castell de Sant Felip

So na Caçana

Torelló

PR Me 2

Camí de Torelló

Camí Vell de Sant Climent

Me-14

PR Me 2

Me-8R

PR Me 2

Cafetería

Me-2

Cala de Sant Esteve

CI-2

Me-12

Calascoves

Binicalaf

PR Me 2

Sant Climent

Me-12

Me-14

Llucmaçanes

Me-8

Marlborough Redoubt

Sant Joan de Binissaida

Torre d'en Penjat

Villa Eugenia

Cala'n Porter

Son Vitamina

aeropuerto

Aeroclub

Binissaida

Camí Sa Torra

Es Caló d'es Vi Blanc

Military area

Me-6

GR 223

Cales Coves

Trebalúger

Trebalúger

Sant Lluís

78

Camí Vell

Camí de Rafalet

Rafalet Vell

Rafalet Petit

Rafalet Nou

Me-8

12

and turns right. The farmhouses of **Binissaida** come into view and the path meets a track (**1h05min**). Turning right, you come on to a tarred lane almost immediately. Follow it to the right,* and pass another fine farmhouse on the left: notice to the left of it that it has its own CHAPEL, even equipped with a bell. Next you will pass on your right the fine FORTIFIED FARM-HOUSE shown below (see also panel page 125).

Five minutes beyond this farmhouse, turn right into Horts de Binissaida along CAMI DE SA

---

*Turning left with the Camí de Cavalls makes a pleasant link with Walk 12; in 10 minutes it would bring you to the 1h08min-point in that walk.

TORRA. In another five minutes, ignore a track to the right and keep ahead on the wider one, to arrive in a further five minutes back at the GATES OF VILLA EUGENIA (**5**). Turn left here and retrace your steps a short way along walled-in CAMI DE SA CALA, past the point where you joined it at **4** after leaving the Torre d'en Penjat.

Continue to follow the Camí de Sa Cala/Camí de Cavalls down to the end of **Cala de Sant Esteve** and rejoin the tarmac road. Turn left and cross the end of the *cala*, but leave the road when you come to a clump of bamboo and go up the little Roman path at **7**. At the top bear left and turn left at the T-junction. Soon you will be back beside the CEMETERY (**1h35min**).

Pick up the notes for Walk 4 on page 50 now, and follow that walk from the 2h17min-point to the 2h55min-point at **9** — the MILITARY MUSEUM in the **Plaça de S'Esplanada**, the square in the centre of **Es Castell**. Walk ahead until you come to CARRER VICTORI. Turn left, pass the CHURCH, and the BUS STOP is to your right (**2h15min**).

Top left: the Military Museum in the Plaça de S'Esplanada in Es Castell; left: Cales Fonts, the waterfront in Es Castell, at dusk; above: fortified farmhouse at Binissaida

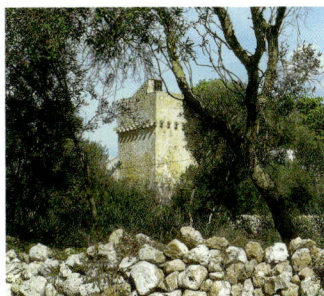

Walk 7: TORELLO AND TALATI DE DALT

See map on reverse of touring
map; see also photos on pages 1,
12, 13, 39
Distance: about 15km/9.3mi;
3h35min
Grade: ● moderate because of
length, few ups and downs
Equipment: comfortable footwear, sunhat, raingear, suncream,
picnic, plenty of water

How to get there and return:
🚌 or 🚗 to Maó; as Walk 1, page
32 (park in the Esplanade Square)
Shorter walk: Torelló (about
12km/7.4mi; 2h55min; grade,
equipment, access as main walk).
Follow the walk to **6** (1h36min),
then turn right and follow the
notes from the 2h15min-point to
the end, *omitting Talatí de Dalt*.

In 1956, 'Torelló' first appeared on the archaeological map of Menorca, when a very large and magnificent mosaic pavement featuring flowers, birds and animals was discovered. It has since been identified as the floor of an early Christian church. Talatí de Dalt, too, is famed among enthusiasts of Menorcan archaeology as one of the most beautiful of talayotic village sites. This walk also visits two other interesting *talayots,* and so is an excellent way for the visitor to see some of Menorca's prehistoric legacy.

Start out by facing the **Monument to the Civil War Dead 1** in the **Plaça de S'Esplanada** (see town plan on pages 36-37). Leave the square by the street in the far right-hand corner, CARRER VASSALLO (it is the airport road, Me-12). Pass the barracks built in the 18th century to house British soldiers and keep ahead at a large roundabout. After passing a sports stadium, you will see ahead a dual carriageway and roundabout. Just before this, turn left along a narrow lane and in 30m turn right and go up steps on to the BRIDGE OVER THE DUAL CARRIAGEWAY. Where the bridge divides, turn left. At the bottom of the bridge, turn round and walk back to the roundabout. Follow the dual carriageway to the right towards Sant Lluís for 100m/yds, then turn right again in the direction of Llucmaçanes and rejoin the little lane. You now follow this lane (**2**; CAMI DE BAIX) for just over 1km. Ignore the turning to the right by No 27.

After an S-bend round a DAIRY FARM, you come to a straight stretch of road. Looking right you may see the fine farmhouse of Sa Cudia, almost hidden behind its imposing palm trees. In a few metres you come to a narrow, walled-in crossing track (**28min**). Turn right and follow this track (the PR Me 2 between Trepucó and Calescoves) for another 1km. Fortunately the drystone walls are sufficiently low to afford a good view of the fields. In them you will see sheds built of loose stones — the way the people of Menorca have been building for three thousand years (see the panel on page 123).

At the end of the track (**43min**) you come to a junction with a road. Turn right. In 350m, at a roundabout, you meet the MAIN ROAD from Maó to the airport at Sant Climent (**3**), the Me-12).

Cross this road carefully, using the pedestrian walkways and crossings; then carry on towards

58

the industrial estate opposite (*Polígon industrial*), *leaving* the PR Me 2. Walk along the left-hand carriageway for under 200m, then turn left down a narrow lane with a no entry sign and a magenta sign, 'TALAIOTS DE CORNIA' (both pointing in the other direction). Fork left when you are in sight of the large farmhouse shown below, **Curnia Vey**, and pass the splendid *talayot* of **Curnia Nou** (**4**) on your left. This is the first megalithic building visitors see on leaving the airport.

After exploring the *talayot,* carry on past a scrapyard, and soon you come to a junction with the Me-14 (**1h**). Cross straight over, heading diagonally left and briefly rejoining the PR Me 2. Soon you will enjoy a fine view across fields to the *talayot* at Torelló. Beyond a handful of houses the road is unsurfaced, then metalled again beyond a farm. When you join a road beside the AIRPORT LANDING LIGHTS, turn right for 20m, then left on a lane with two magenta signs announcing 'Torelló'. Ignore

a lane on the left in 250m and, in a further 200m, you will arrive at the towering *talayot* of **Torelló** (**5**; **1h17min**), unusual in that it has an entrance. Continue along the lane. To your left is the omni-present Monte Toro. In six minutes turn right along a short track towards a large shed-like structure, signposted '**Basílica des Fornàs de Torelló**'. It covers the mosaic floor of a church built during the Roman empire. The flowers and animals are African (what a wonderful lion), suggesting that the Menorcan church at this time maintained close links with the church in North Africa, where the great St Augustine was bishop of Hippo.

Return to the lane, turn right and continue in your original direction. After 500m, at a T- JUNCTION (**6**; **1h36min**), turn left along a track — the PR Me 1 between Dalt Sant Joan and Alcaidús — just before a short access road left to a defunct factory, now another scrapyard. Ignore a walled-in track off right in 300m,

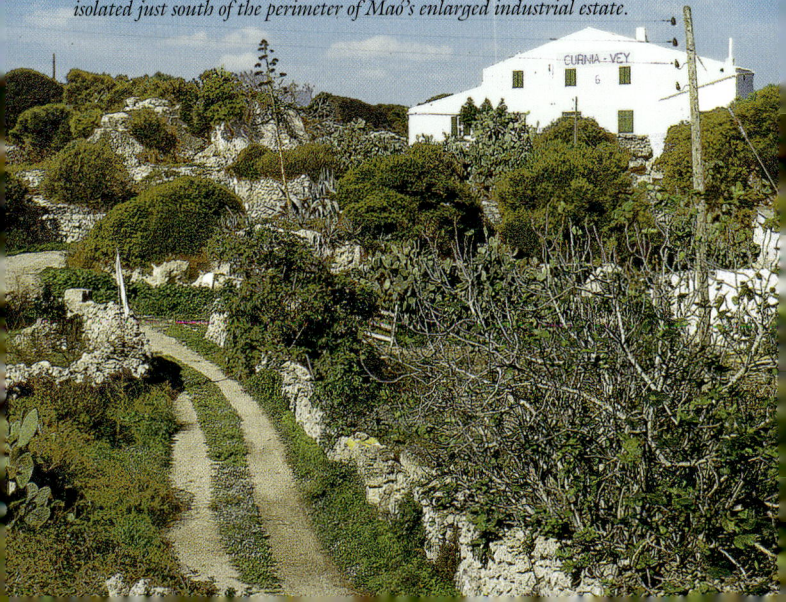

Curnia Vey farmhouse: not only is the track to it metalled, but the farm now stands isolated just south of the perimeter of Maó's enlarged industrial estate.

and follow the track you are on for 700m — to a T-junction with a metalled road. Shortly before the T-junction there is a short section where the track still retains its original Roman paving (see panel page 63).

Turn left, to quickly reach **Talatí de Dalt** (**7**; **1h55min**) — the site of the prehistoric village shown on pages 1 and 12-13. An entrance fee is payable, but it is well worth it (see www.menorca web.net/talati). It is a marvellous place for a picnic (Picnic 5), with ample shade and enough room to get out of the way of other sightseers.

When you leave the talayotic settlement (**2h**), turn right, and after a few metres, turn right again, to retrace your steps to the T-junction at the 1h36min-point (**6**; **2h15min**).

Now you have a choice. You can return to town by following Walk 8 from **6** (page 64), but this means going back over much of your outward route. I think it's preferable to join Walk 3 (even if you've done it already). Turn *left* at this junction, following signs for Maó and Ciutadella. Pass under the Me-14 connecting the Me-1 with the airport and, in 150m, keep left at the fork. Meeting the Me-1, either take the track directly opposite (the PR Me 1) or the one 180m/yds to the right. Both descend to a T-junction by a MEADOW (**2h35min**), where you join Walk 3 just south of **7**. Turning right, use the notes from the 1h25min-point on page 46 to walk back to the **Plaça de S'Esplanada** (**3h35min**).

TALATÍ DE DALT

Talatí de Dalt has all the usual features of these prehistoric Menorcan villages — caves, hypostyle chambers, *talayot*, and *taula*. And all this in an idyllic setting (Picnic 5).

In the absence of metals and large trees, the lives of the ancient villagers were dominated by stones. Looking about you, it is apparent how all their building was done with them, but so also was their hunting and fighting (see opposite).

PREHISTORIC WEAPONRY

The weapon of the Balearic islanders of pre-history was the sling shot. So skilled were they, that they were in great demand as mercenaries for several centuries. When the Carthaginian general Mago sailed into Maó harbour in 206 BC, thereby bequeathing it his name, it was to impress 2000 Menorcan slingers into his army. (It is possible that the very name 'Balearic' comes from the Greek word 'ballein' which means 'to sling'.) Each soldier carried three slings of different sizes, to be used according to the distance, like golf clubs. The stones they used generally weighed about 500g (about a pound), and it was claimed that they were accurate up to 600 paces. Boys were trained from early childhood. Their mothers would place the children's meals up in a tree, and the youngsters had to knock them down with a sling shot. Or go hungry. Their skeletal remains

Photographs: taula *enclosure and* talayot *at the site of Talatí de Dalt (top); the* taula *and nearby standing stones (above)*

show remarkable development of the shoulder-blade and upper humerus, the latter also being bowed.

Having served with the Carthaginian armies, Menorcan slingers later saw service with the Roman legions. Julius Caesar refers to the part they played in his defeat of the Gauls at Alesia in 52 BC.

Walk 8: AN ARCHAEOLOGICAL RAMBLE

See map on reverse of touring map; see also photos on pages 1, 12-13, 39, 60-61 and opposite
Distance: 14km/8.7mi; 3h20min
Grade: easy; basically a long gentle descent on lanes and tracks
Equipment: comfortable footwear, sunhat, raingear, suncream, picnic, plenty of water

How to get there: 🚌 to Alaior or Cala'n Porter, then 🚕 taxi to Torralba d'en Salort.
To return: 🚌 or 🚕 from Maó *Or* leave your car at the end of the walk, beneath Esplanade Square, then go on by bus as above. *Or* park at Torralba (39° 54.733'N, 4° 9.868'E) and take a taxi back.

Since this walk takes in two major prehistoric settlements, two additional important *talayots*, two *navetas*, the mosaic floor of a Roman church, and follows what was the main road across the island until Sir Richard Kane built his new highway early in the 18th century, it is clearly a 'must' for the amateur historian and archaeology buff.

Start out at the prehistoric settlement of **Torralba d'en Salort** (**1**), inhabited for two millennia from 1800 BC. Hoskin and Waldron suggest that the *taula* precinct is the most beautiful prehistoric monument in the Balearics, and date it from 890 BC. At the foot of the *taula* were found a small stone altar and a bronze bull. Nearby is the **Pou de Na Patarra**, a huge well 50m/160ft deep, dating from 800 BC, with nine flights of steps

leading down, and a handrail hewn out of the rock.

Some 20m/yds beyond the site car park, turn left on a track by the side of Torralba d'en Salort rental villa. This track, the CAMI D'ALCAIDUS, was once the main road across Menorca; it's continuation, via Alaior, is now a busy road. Proceed through gorgeous farming country for 2km, until you pass on your right the drive to SANTA ELISABET (**39min**), then

Hoskin and Waldron suggest that the taula *precinct is the most beautiful prehistoric monument in the Balearics.*

SANT RAFAEL on your left. Ignore a track to the right here. In five minutes you come to a tarmac road and, when you do, look out for two picturesque OLD WELLS (**2**) — one on your left with a wheel and buckets, and another on your right. Notice too the curious single standing stone inscribed '90 ANYS' (years). Follow the road round to the left. Where you pass beneath power lines there is a road on your right, but ignore that for the moment, because here you make a short detour to two *navetas*. Turn left and walk 50m to the Me-1. Cross with care and walk along the road opposite. The well-signposted *navetas* of **Rafal Rubí** (**3**; **56min**) were built in the talayotic period as burial chambers.

When you leave the *navetas*, walk back along the lane to the Me-1 and cross over. This time take the road on the left when you reach the junction, joining the PR Me 1. Keep going along this road for 1.5km/1mi, until you reach the hamlet of **Algendar de Sa Costa** (**4**), and turn left at the crossroads. Ignore any signs for 'Talatí de Dalt' until, after about 20 minutes, you come to its small roadside car parking area and entrance. You join Walk 7 — and its waypoints — here at **Talatí de Dalt** (**7**; **1h43min**; Picnic 5), another prehistoric village in a lovely setting,. Walk 7 will tell you more about the inhabitants of these townships.

Continue along the road in the same direction for 100 metres, then turn right along a track, the CAMI VELL D'ALAIOR ('Old Alaior Road'; still Walk 7 and the PR Me 1). A little way along this track you come upon a section of very fine paving — a clue to the Roman

ROMAN ROADS

Wheeled vehicles need smooth, flat surfaces if they are to work efficiently. An uneven surface not only gives an uncomfortable ride, but every bump acts as a brake on the vehicle's progress. The Romans managed to obtain remarkably smooth surfaces by taking meticulous care over the shaping and laying of the cobbles with which their roads were surfaced.

The 140 km of roads they built on Menorca were no exception. Today most of the old Roman roads are buried beneath later resurfacing. But not quite everywhere, and a few stretches of Roman paving still lie on the surface, and you will walk over several of them as you follow the routes in this book.

The best and longest stretch is to be found on Picnic 8, part of the path leading up to the ruins of the summer palace of the Moorish king of Menorca at the time of the Reconquest. Formerly there had been a Roman fortress here. Other lengths of Roman paving will be encountered on Walks 3, 4, 6, 7 and 8.

Photograph: Roman road at Santa Agueda (Picnic 8)

63

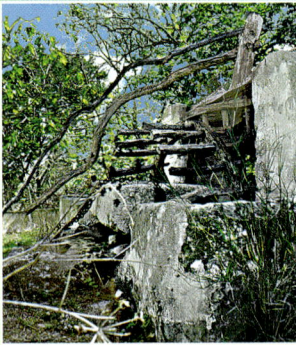

WELLS

On Menorca it seems that no matter where you look, you see a well (*pou* in Menorcan).

Perhaps that is an exaggeration, but they are very plentiful and you will see many, beside paths and in fields.

The simple stone structures surrounding them, sometimes adding drinking troughs, are often curiously attractive and the wells add much interest to the scenery.

Photo: well near the farm of Sant Rafael

Return to the lane and carry on in the same direction for six minutes, when you will reach the *talayot* of **Torelló** (**5**; also called 'Torellonet Vell'; **2h22min**). It is unusual in that it has an entrance leading to a chamber on top. In 200m you join the PR Me 2 and ignore a lane on the right (the Camí de Mussulá). Three minutes later emerge on a road beside the AIRPORT LANDING LIGHTS. Turn right, but after 20m turn left on a lane (still the PR Me 2); it is metalled at first, but after a farm reverts to an older and simpler state for a short time. After 10 minutes cross a main road (the Me-14) and go along a facing lane (CAMI VELL DE SANT CLIMENT), pass a scrapyard, and ignore a turning on the right.

Now you will see the fine **Curnia Nou** *talayot* on your right (**4**; **2h43min**). Keep ahead past some large CAVES. As you approach a T-junction, you should have the view of Curnia Vey farmhouse shown on page 59 — sitting isolated at the perimeter of Maó's ever-growing industrial estate (*Polígon industrial*). Turn right at the junction. Follow the lane to the right and join a road. Turn right.

Walk towards the main road, but turn left just short of it, and follow the quieter road (CARRER DE ARTRUTX) the length of the industrial estate into Maó. At the end of the industrial estate, cross the DUAL CARRIAGEWAY at the zebra and then the footbridge over the carrigeway (**3h11min**), to keep ahead past a sports ground. When you come to another ROUNDABOUT, keep straight on (after crossing the road on zebras) and follow CARRER VASSALLO to the **Plaça de S'Esplanada** in Maó (**1**; **3h20min**).

origins of this road. Of course, linking as it does so many Bronze Age towns, the way itself predates by far the Roman era. Five minutes along the track, look on your right for a narrow path which leads to some CAVES. Some 200m further on you are directly beneath the airport flight path.

In some 200m, at a signposted T-junction, turn right along a metalled lane, the CAMI DE TORELLÓ (**6**; **2h03min**). Soon afterwards, beyond an old QUARRY, turn left along a short track bearing a magenta-coloured sign, '**Basílica des Fornàs de Torelló**'. This brings you to a Roman mosaic pavement, believed to be the floor of a Christian church. (See the notes on page 60.)

Walk 9: THREE WALKS NEAR THE VALLEY OF EGYPT

Walk a: From Sant Llorenç to Binimatzoc (7km/4.5mi; 1h40min; ● easy, on lanes and tracks)

Walk b: From Sant Llorenç to Ejipte (2.8km/1.7mi; 50min; ● easy track walking)

Walk c: Sant Llorenç and Puig Menor (6km/3.7mi; 1h35min; ● easy, but with a final ascent of 90m/250ft)

Equipment: comfortable footwear, sunhat, suncream, raingear, picnic, plenty of water

How to get there and return: Only by 🚗: drive along the Camí d'en Kane until you are nearly level with Alaior. You will come to a crossroads where one turning is to Alaior and the other is signposted to Camí de Binixems. Follow the latter road for about 3 kilometres (2 miles), when you will come to a junction with the Camí d'en Rossi (or Rus) on the left. Either park here or continue along the Camí de Binixems for another 500m until you are nearly at the church of Sant Llorenç and park at a small clearing on your right at 1 (39° 57.458'N, 4° 11.109'E).

Here are three very pleasant inland walks along lanes or stone cart tracks through a lovely and fairly isolated part of the island known as 'Es Custe de Egipte'. The vistas are bucolic rather than impressive, but the wooded sections offer shady picnic spots on hot days.

Start Walk a near the little church of **Sant Llorenç** (1) by walking back to the junction with the Camí d'en Rossi (or Rus) and turning along this road. Follow it past the turning into the Santa Margalida property, until you arrive at a Y-junction (**15min**), where you turn right. The tarmac ends (**23min**) and you go through a gate, keeping left at a fork in 50m. In three minutes go through another gate. The track loops round the bottom of the hill below the ESTANCIA DE SANT PERE for ten minutes, before you go through a gateway (**36min**). Three minutes later fork left to avoid BINIMATZOC farmhouse, and in four minutes go through a gate. The track now runs through trees. At the next fork go right, ignoring a gateway on the left. Soon you will have a good view over the last field before the Me-7 road, and unless you are going to pick up transport there, turn back here (2; **50min**).

Retrace your steps now. Ignore the gateway on the right, walk through woodland for a couple of minutes, then go through a gate and, four minutes after that, turn right at the T-junction where the track on the left goes to the farm of Binimatzoc. In three minutes go through another gate (**59min**). On top of a hill on your left you can see the farm of SANT PERE, and your track will loop round the bottom of the hill. After ten minutes, when you are about three-quarters of the way round the loop, you go through yet another gate. In three minutes bear right, ignoring the track on the left which goes to the farm (**1h13min**). A minute later you pass through the final gate and the track becomes a metalled lane. In eight minutes keep straight ahead at a junction, ignoring a road to the right, on what is now a wider road. You pass the entrance to ESTANCIA DE SANTA MARGALIDA in another seven minutes (**1h29min**) and after a similar interval you will

65

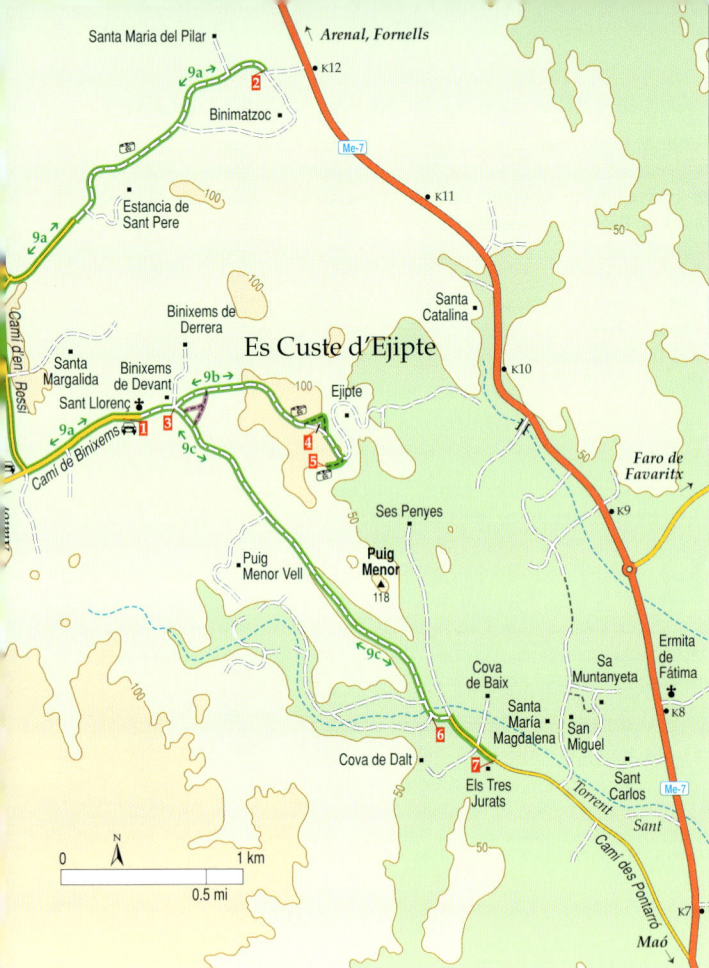

Santa Maria del Pilar •

↑ *Arenal, Fornells*

9a • K12

2

Binimatzoc •

Me-7

• K11

•
Estancia de
Sant Pere

100

9a

Cami d'en Rossi

Binixems de
Derrera

Santa
Catalina •

Es Custe d'Ejipte

• K10

Santa
Margalida

Binixems
de Devant

9b →

100

Ejipte •

Sant Llorenç ♦

9a →

1 **3**

9c →

Cami de Binixems

4

5

Faro de
Favaritx

• K9

50

Ses Penyes

•

Puig
Menor Vell

**Puig
Menor**

▲
118

9c →

Cova
de Baix

Sa
Muntanyeta •

Ermita
de Fátima
♦

• K8

Santa
María
Magdalena •

San
Miguel •

Cova de Dalt •

6

7

Els Tres
Jurats

Sant
Carlos
•

Me-7

100

50

Torrent

Sant

Cami des Pontarro

N

0   1 km

0.5 mi

50

Maó
↘

• K7

come to the junction with Camí de
Binixems. Turn left for 500m/yds
to arrive at **Sant Llorenç**
(**1h40min**).

Start Walk b at **1** by walking
along the lane from the little
church of **Sant Llorenç** for five
minutes, until you come to a
crossroads beside the farm of
BINIXEMS DE DEVANT (**3**). Your
ongoing route is straight ahead,
following a track through a gate
and across a field. This gate is is
usually locked, so look for a stile in
the wall anywhere from 20m to
100m downhill (it keeps moving!).
Once over the stile, join the
CART TRACK on the far side of the

gate. Be aware that much of this
area is private property, and you
will not be able to go all the way to
the Egipte houses.

After about 15min you will
come to another LOCKED GATE
(**4**). Here you must retrace steps
for up to 30m to find the 'bypass'
path on your right. The path
rejoins the track. As you go
forward now, you will see the
Ejipte farmhouse on your left and,
just before the track bends sharply
left to begin to descend, the valley
of **Ses Penyes**. The hill of Puig
Menor stands out on the right. Do
not follow the track downhill, but
continue to walk round to the

right, for the view over the GORGE (**5**; **25min**).

Turn back now and retrace your steps. After 15 minutes you should see on the other side of a little field the path that will take you up and round to the right and bring you back to the stile in the wall. Once back on the lane, turn right to return to **Sant Llorenç** (**50min**).

Start Walk c at the parking area (**1**); pass the church of **Sant Llorenç**, and continue along the **Camí de Binixems** for five minutes, until you come to a crossroads beside the farm of BINIXEMS DE DEVANT. Turn right and follow the lane downhill. In ten minutes you pass the entrance to PUIG MENOR VELL farm on your right. At the bottom of the hill ignore a farm entrance on the right, and in 100m turn left at a

T-junction (**6**). Walk beside the **Torrent Sant** for another 100m, then turn right. Although a handful of cars may pass, almost all will belong to the local land-owners, approaching from the nearby Me-7. So you can enjoy the flora and birdsong of this gentle countryside in peace.

Pass between the farms of COVA DE DALT (Upper Cova) and COVA DE BAIX (Lower Cova) and lastly that of the three Councillors — ELS TRES JURATS (**7**). Can you see the rocks that gave the farm its name on your right in solemn contemplation (**45min**)? The rest of the way from here to its junction with the Me-7 has little of interest, and unless you are intending to pick up transport there, turn back now and retrace your steps uphill back to **Sant Llorenç** (**1h35min**).

The Ejipte farmhouse in Es Custe d'Ejipte

Distance: 13.8km/8.6mi; 3h35min
Grade: fairly strenuous, with an ascent/descent of 275m/900ft
Equipment: comfortable footwear, sunhat, raingear, suncream, picnic, plenty of water
How to get there and return:
🚌 to Alaior or 🚍 to Es Mercadal (park in the town centre), then 🚌 to Alaior
To return: 🚌 or 🚍 from Es Mercadal
Shorter walk: Es Mercadal — Monte Toro — Es Mercadal (7km/ 4.3mi; 2h20min; equipment and grade as above (ascent of 280m/ 1000ft; access: 🚌 or 🚍 to Es Mercadal; park near the bus stop at 39° 59.112'N, 4° 5.679'E). From Es Mercadal walk back to the nearby ring road road (Me-1) and follow it towards Maó. At the roundabout, turn left on the Camí d'en Kane. Follow it uphill for 1km (about 20 minutes), then join the main walk at **5** (the 1h53min-point).
Alternative endings. The road up Mount Toro is very busy these days. You may be deterred by the final steep climb or by the traffic

on a comparatively narrow road. Here are three alternative ways to finish the walk.
1   Avoiding the climb to the summit and the traffic. At the 1h53min-point (**5**), do not turn right, but continue along the Camí d'en Kane as it descends to Es Mercadal. Turn right at the junction with the Me-1 ring road and follow it to the right for 130m, then turn left to the bus stop (**7**).
2   Avoiding the climb to the summit. At the 2h16min-point (the Monte Toro–Es Mercadal road), turn left and descend it to Es Mercadal, then follow the notes after the 3h30min-point.
3   Avoiding some of the traffic. Follow the walk to the summit and head back downhill. When you come back to the entrance to the farm of Rafal d'es Frares (your outward route), turn left. Turn right on the track just before the farmhouse and, when you reach the junction with the Camí d'en Kane, turn right and use the notes for Alternative ending 1 above.

Every visitor will wish to get to the summit of Monte Toro, Menorca's loftiest hill (at 358m/1175ft, it just merits its name 'mountain'). The easiest way is to drive up. For the energetic, this walk provides an enjoyable alternative combining an interesting country walk with an easier climb (at least as far as the 200m contour), than the road from Es Mercadal offers.

The town of Alaior is the third largest on Menorca. It was founded soon after the Reconquest in 1304 by King James II of Mallorca, on the site of the farmhouse of Ihalor. The start of my route is intended to show you some attractive corners of the town, that some claim to be the prettiest on the island. The parish church of Santa Eulalia, fortified in 1558 after both Maó and Ciuta-

della had been sacked by Turkish pirates, and the 17th-century Franciscan convent arc of special interest. Alaior is best known for its ice cream, but shoes and cheese are made here too.
   The BUS STOP/CAR PARK (**1**) in **Alaior** is in CARRER SANT JOAN BAPTISTA DE LA SALLE, in front of a park and playground. Facing the park, **begin the walk** by turning left, then turning right along the

The convent on Monte Toro, with its tower and chapel (above), statue of Christ (right) and the entrance (far right)

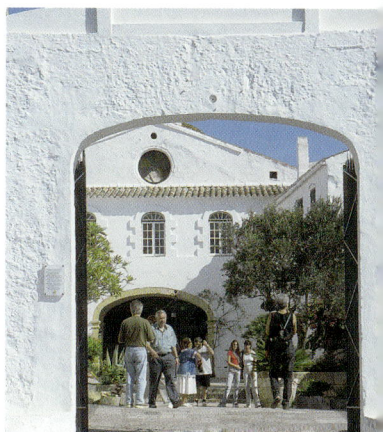

street running along the left-hand side of the park, CARRER MESTRE DURAN. The large building ahead dates from 1624. Originally a Franciscan convent, its pink church was dedicated to San Diego (St James). The local people refer to it as Sa Lluna, and it has now been converted to housing. Turn left in front of it along CARRER LES ESCOLES, then turn right and pass its entrance — turn in to look at the picturesque cloister.

Turn right and follow CARRER SANT DIEGO along its west wall, forking right at the end to go downhill. Turn left at the end, then fork right up CARRER COSTA D'ES POU. Bear right along CARRER DEL BISBE GONYALONS. At the top, cross CARRER D'ES PORRASSAR VELL and go straight ahead up CARRER DE SES NUVIES. At the top of the hill, Santa Eulalia's church is

on your right. Turn right and walk in front of the church along CARRER DES RETXATS. Continue round until this joins CARRER DE SES GUIXES. Turn right, and in 50m/yds you are back at CARRER D'ES PORRASSAR VELL, by a palm tree. Turn left. After 100m, past the side of a tiny square, the **Plaça Nova**, turn right into ES CAMI NOU. Pass a small garden with a playground and the CHURCH beside it (**2**; **16min**), and you have now crossed Alaior.

Turn left along a metalled track/cycle trail at the back of the church. Ignore the first turn-off to the left in 100m, but in two minutes turn left along the second one, the CAMI DE BINIGUARDA. Keep to this narrow track, ignoring any turn-offs to farms or houses. Eventually, after a little over 1km, the metalled lane bears left to some properties; keep straight ahead on a track here. There should be a sign for a cycle route. This track was the main road before Kane's road was built. After going under power lines you begin to walk through woodland. When you come out of the wood, go under power lines, cross over a stream and turn right at a T-junction (turning left would bring you to the main road). Cycle route 5 is signed here for 'Es Mercadal' (**3**; **1h08min**).

Some 14 minutes after the T-junction you meet another junction, this time with a metalled road. This is the CAMI D'EN KANE (**4**), which from here to Es Mercadal follows the same line as the older road. Turn left and follow it for half an hour, passing three large farms: S'ASTANSIA, BINI LLOBET and S'ARANJASSA. After the last of these the road goes downhill and bends to the left.

Ignore a track to the right on the bend which leads to the farm of Sant Joan de la Creu, but within 50m turn right through a gate (**5**; **1h53min**). *(The Shorter walk joins here.)* Climb a track past the drive to SON CARLOS farm and in 12 minutes turn right towards the farm of RAFAL D'ES FRARES on a cart track. Go through a gate, and follow the track round to the left. Keep ahead at the end of the track, and turn left at a T-junction along a tarmac drive, leaving the farmhouse off to your right. Walk up the side of a valley, go over a cattle grid and join the ES MERCADAL – MONTE TORO road (**2h16min**).

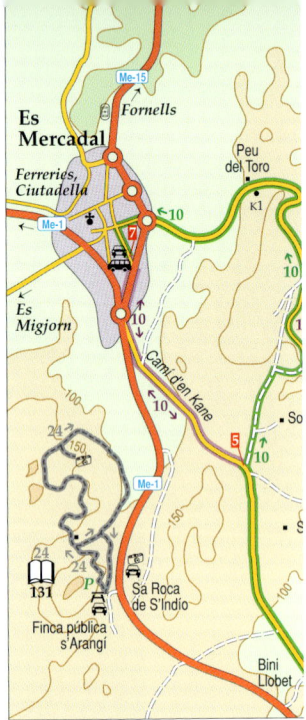

Turn right and wind up the hillside. It is just about wide enough for you to keep out of the way of traffic. It will take you about 45 minutes to climb to the summit of **Monte Toro** (**6**; **2h50min**). The 17th-century convent buildings house a cafeteria and toilets, as well as a gift shop. Outside, the statue of Christ gazes a little forlornly, I fancy, at the emblems of the more recent gods of the 21st century.

Your descent is very much quicker! Keep to the side of the road, facing the oncoming traffic, and you should be at the ROUNDABOUT at the foot of the hill in 40 minutes (**3h30min**). Go straight over the roundabout and enter **Es Mercadal**. You will come to a little square: cross it and turn left. Follow the street nearly to the end, where the BUS STOP is on your left (**7**; **3h35min**).

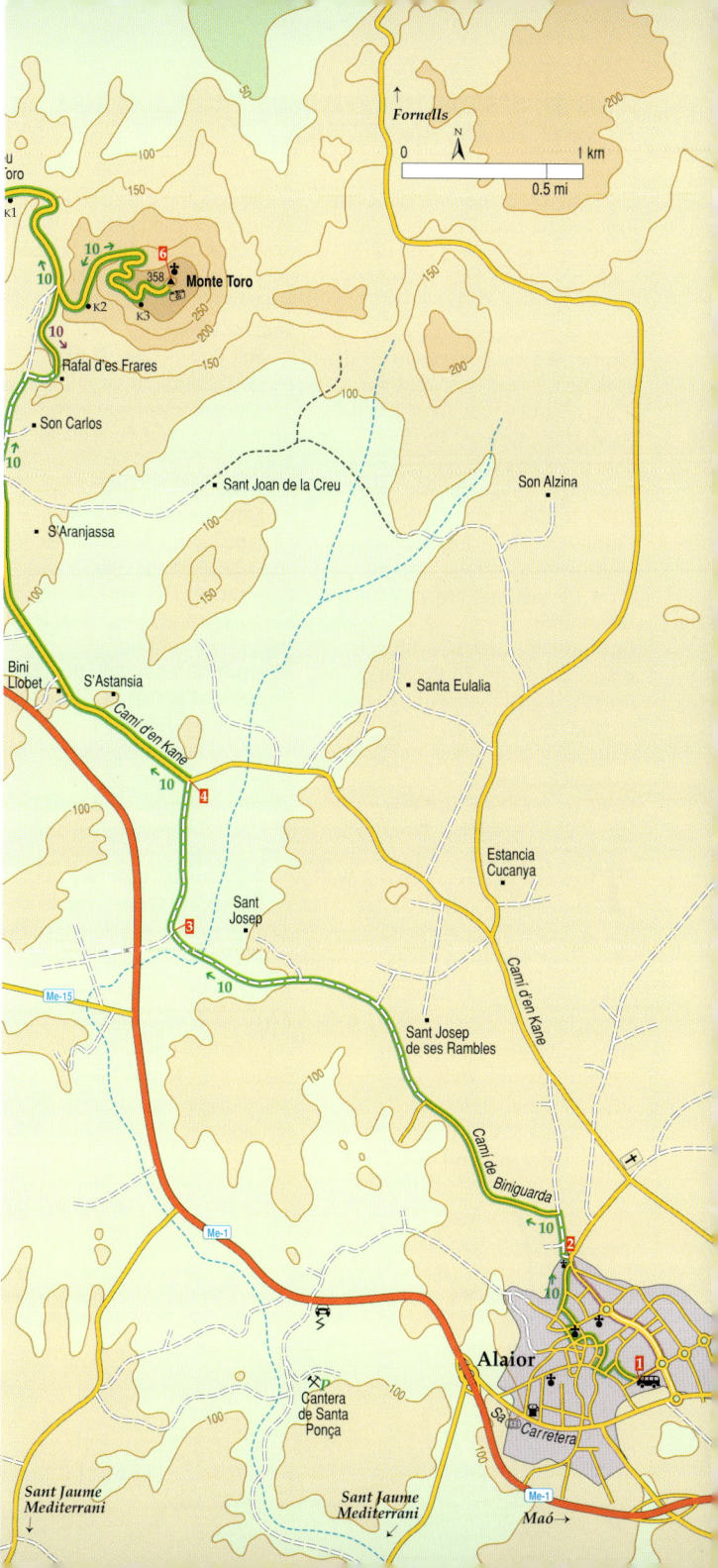

↑
Fornells

N

0   1 km

0.5 mi

10 →

10

6

358 ▲ **Monte Toro**

к1

10

к2   к3

10

■ Rafal d'es Frares

■ Son Carlos

10

■ Sant Joan de la Creu

■ Son Alzina

■ S'Aranjassa

Bini Llobet

■ S'Astansia

Camí d'en Kane

■ Santa Eulalia

10

4

Estancia Cucanya

3

Sant Josep

10

Me-15

Camí d'en Kane

■ Sant Josep de ses Rambles

Camí de Biniguarda

Me-1

10

2

10

Cantera de Santa Ponça

Alaior

1

Sa Carretera

Sant Jaume Mediterrani

Sant Jaume Mediterrani

Me-1

Maó →

Walk 11: BESIDE THE REED BEDS: FROM SON BOU TO SANT TOMAS AND RETURN

Distance: 10.4km/6.5mi; 3h25min (*Note:* no time has been included for exploring the caves mentioned at the very end of the walk, nor for walking to and from the bus stop to the starting point at the beach car park.)

Grade: ● easy, but remember that walking through sand dunes is tiring. Avoid windy days, when the beach route through the sand dunes can be unpleasant. (If a windy day is unavoidable, you may prefer to follow the Camí de Cavalls to/from Punta Radona — see violet lines on the map and allow for ups and downs of about 100m/300ft.)

Equipment: sandals, sunhat, swimwear, towel, suncream, picnic (or have lunch in one of the many restaurants en route), plenty of water, binoculars, bird and flower recognition books

How to get there and return: 🚌 or 🚗 to/from Son Bou. Walk

from the bus stop down the road to the beach and turn right. Motorists should park in the large car park to the right of the road at the rear of the beach (39° 54.016'N, 4° 4.386'E).

Shorter walks
1 Son Bou — Sant Tomàs (4.5km/2.8mi; 1h35min; ● grade, equipment and access as main walk). End the walk in Sant Tomàs and return by bus or taxi from the Es Broc restaurant.
2 Sant Tomàs — Son Bou (4.5km/2.8mi; 1h35min; ● grade and equipment as main walk). Start the walk in Sant Tomàs if you are staying there, and take a taxi back from Son Bou.

Alternative walk: Son Bou, Sant Tomàs and Binigaus. Since Walk 13 starts and finishes in Sant Tomàs, this walk can be combined with Walk 13. See page 79 for details of ● grade and equipment, and to estimate distance/time.

This is a gentle, relaxing walk for naturalists (and indeed for naturists), at first along a part of the coast where in all likelihood you will see more flowers and birds than anywhere else on Menorca, and then along what are easily Menorca's longest and best beaches. It is most definitely a walk for a sunny day.

Begin at the CAR PARK (**1**) at **Son Bou**: leave by the exit on the western side and walk towards the sea. Do not go to the beach, but bear right and follow a roped-off path behind the sand dunes and beside the reed beds. The marsh or

LAGOON on your right is the outstanding physical feature of San Jaime/**Sant Jaume Mediterrani** and a magnet for bird life. There is nothing else like it on Menorca. You briefly join the beach to walk around its oulet to the sea, until

Lagoon and marsh at Sant Jaume Mediterrani (top and above); Son Bou beach (left; Picnic 18)

you can take another boardwalk inland. Then keep to the path for the next 35 minutes (two kilometres).

At the end of the marsh the path brings you to a GATE IN A WALL (**2**; **35min**). Beyond is tiny

elevation known as **Punta Radona**. Beyond this headland you join the Camí de Cavalls (**3**) and come to the **Platja de Sant Tomàs**, beside the Hotel Victoria Playa (**4**; **1h05min**). You will want to explore **Sant Tomàs**, and there are three ways to cross it: you can walk along the beach; walk behind the beach and in front of the hotels on a little promenade; or walk along the main street. Whichever you choose, when you come to the Es Bruc restaurant at the end of the Me-18 road from Es Migjorn (**5**; **1h35min**).

From here retrace your steps to **Punta Radona** (**3**; **2h35min**). From here you have a choice. Either go back the way you came, follow the Camí de Cavalls or, for a change, walk back on the hard sand, stopping

for a swim en route (as I do).

Back at the car park at **Son Bou** (**1**; **3h10min**), do not stop, but carry on walking. First of all you pass a delightful picnic spot shaded by pine trees (Picnic 18) and then come to the ruins of an ancient Christian church (**6**) built during the Roman Empire. Of interest is the baptismal font carved out of a single stone in the shape of a four-leaf clover. From here you could press on a short way for a closer look at the caves in the cliff ahead. Son Bou boasts one of the largest collections of prehistoric caves on the island (for more information about such caves, see the panel on page 126). Then return to the car park at **Son Bou** (**3h25min**).

Flowering fields near Son Bou

Walk 12: THROUGH THE DEEP SOUTH

See also photo on page 4
Distance: 12km/7.5mi; 3h
Grade: easy, mostly on good
paths, tracks and roads; no appreciable ascents/descents — but there
is a bit of scrambling above Caló
d'es Rafalet
Equipment: comfortable footwear, sunhat, raingear, swimwear,
towel, suncream, picnic (or lunch
at a restaurant en route), plenty of
water
How to get there: 🚌 to Sant
Lluís or 🚗 to Punta Prima (park
near the bus stop at 39° 48.808'N,
4° 16.720'E), then 🚌 to Sant Lluís
To return: 🚌 or 🚗 from Punta
Prima

Shorter walks
1 S'Algar — Punta Prima
(4.5km/2.8mi; 1h10min; grade,
equipment, return as main walk;
access: 🚌 to S'Algar). From the
bus stop, walk down to the
seafront, turn right and follow the
main walk from the 1h58min-
point at 🟥9 to the end.
2 Trebalúger and Rafalet
(8km/5mi; 2h; grade, equipment
as main walk; access: 🚌 or 🚗 to
Sant Lluís; *return:* 🚌 from
S'Algar). Follow the main walk to
the 1h58min-point at 🟥9, then turn
right and walk uphill to the bus
stop in the centre of S'Algar; alight
in Sant Lluís if you parked there.

This is a walk of contrasting scenery. At first meandering
through farming country, it later follows the coastline, visiting the delightful holiday resorts of S'Algar, Alcaufar and Punta
Prima. The town of Sant Lluís was built by the French during
their seven-year occupation of Menorca from 1756 to 1763. The
king of France being Louis XV, the church here was dedicated
by the French (Galli) to St Louis (Divo Ludovico) in 1760, as
the inscription across the front proudly proclaims. Hence the
name of the town. The interior of the church, though simple, is
worth a visit before you start your walk. Also of interest is the
windmill in the centre of town, near the bus stop, which has
been converted into a museum of ethnology.

The walk begins in the little
square, the **Plaça Nova** in the
centre of **Sant Lluís**, beside the
BUS STOP (🟥1). Standing with your
back to the square and facing the
windmill shown overleaf, turn left
and walk away from it southwards
along CARRER DE SANT LLUIS.
Turn down the second street on
the left, CARRER DE SANT ANTONI,
passing the church on your right,
and continue straight across a dual
carriageway. Follow the country
lane, the CAMÍ REIAL D'ES POU
NOU, for 15 minutes. On your left
you may glimpse the imposing
talayot of Trebalúger through
breaks in the trees. When you

come to a T-junction before the
farm of RAFALETO, turn left along
a walled-in track, the CAMI VELL
DE TREBALUGER (🟥2; **23min**), and
ignore any side-turnings.
  After ten minutes you will
arrive at the village of **Trebalúger**,
where the Camí Vell de Trebalúger
becomes metalled. Two minutes
later turn briefly right at a
T-junction in front of a house, then
almost immediately left, still on the
Camí Vell de Trebalúger, ignoring
streets to the right. In three
minutes turn left into CAMI D'ES
TALAIOT by the magenta sign
'**Talaiot de Trebalúger**', to come
to this fine cyclopean building (🟥3;

75

41min). Unlike most *talayots* today, this one has steps up to an entrance, beyond which is the walled enclosure.

On leaving the *talayot*, retrace your steps to the Camí Vell de Trebalúger and turn right. When you come to a T-junction, turn left into CARRER DE SA TORRE. Ignore two streets on the right, then turn right into CAMI DE RAFALET (**4**). Stay on this road as it winds through the village. You will pass many side streets; ignore them. Fifteen minutes after leaving the *talayot* you will walk out of the village, passing power lines and a TRANSFORMER on your left. After three minutes ignore a track on the right leading to the farm of RAFALET PETIT but, three minutes later (just before you come to a farm building), look left: in the distance you will see a circle of military AERIAL MASTS and, perhaps, between the trees, the tower of a medieval fortified farmhouse at Binissaida (seen at close quarters on Walk 6; photograph page 57). Ignore another track to the right on a bend. In three minutes the lane bends left, then right, to the entrance to SON VIDAL farmhouse. A gravity gate at the right of the their access track gives access to the CAMÍ DE CAVALLS (**5**): follow

the path across fields to the gates of the RAFALET NOU farm. Keeping to the *Camí,* cross more farmland until you join the Rafalet track by a pylon. Follow this track (still the Camí de Cavalls) to the right until after about 50m the track bends to the left. Leave the *Camí* here, and go through a gap in a wall on your left, down beside the **Barranc de Rafalet** (**6**; **1h24min**). The path runs through a wood of mainly holly oaks for six minutes. At the end of the path is the delightful setting for Picnic 14. On your right, in the corner, is a tiny path up which you will continue. But not before you have pressed forward to discover the minuscule **Caló d'es Rafalet** (**7**).

Return to the path and, after a short scramble, bear left at the top of the cliff. Follow one of the paths beside the creek to the end. All paths lead ultimately to the same place, where a stile *(botador)* takes you over a wall to the ROAD (**8**). Turn left and walk down the road beside the sea. At the bottom of the hill, follow the road where it bends right, but then take the first left down to the sea and turn right along the promenade.

At the end of the promenade, keep left and walk between S'ALGAR DIVING CENTRE (**9**;

1h58min) and the sea. *(Shorter walk 1 joins here; Shorter walk 2 turns right.)* Continue between the sea on your left and a swimming pool/ restaurant on your right, towards a line of SMALL WHITE POSTS (**2h**). Go through a gap and turn right. When you come to a wall, turn left and follow a well-walked path along the coast for five minutes, to a road. Turn right; 'PLAYA/BEACH' is written on the wall ahead. The road bends left to a T-junction, where you turn right. Follow this street and make your way down to the beach of **Alcaufar**.

Cross the beach and go through a gate on the far side. The Camí de Cavalls, just above you, now follows a path to the left and uphill. Ignore paths which descend to the water's edge. The *Camí* leads you round a headland and past tiny **Caló Roig**. After some 16 minutes on the *Camí,* leave it briefly, to rise up to a WATCH-TOWER above Caló Roig (**10**; **2h30min**). On leaving the watchtower, rejoin the *Camí* and follow the path southwest along the coast for half an hour. To your left is **Illa de l'Aire**.

It was in May 1756 that Admiral John Byng had his ill-fated encounter with the French fleet in these waters. The British garrison in Fort St Philip had been besieged for two months by a French army commanded by the Duc de Richelieu that had come ashore at Ciutadella. Eighty-two year old General Blakeney waited for the Royal Navy to relieve his men. At last the garrison saw the fleet arrive. Out sailed the Marquis

From top to bottom: Caló d'es Rafalet; windmill housing the ethnological museum at Sant Lluís; Sant Lluís church

de Galissonière to engage it, but soon withdrew into Maó harbour. Then, to the horror of the defenders, the British fleet turned about and sailed back to Gibraltar. Blakeney surrendered, and for seven years Britain was without a Mediterranean naval base. Byng was court-martialled at Portsmouth. Found guilty of negligence, he was executed by firing squad on board a captured French vessel, the Monarque, on 14th March the following year, 'pour encourager les autres,' as Voltaire wryly observed in *Candide*.

On reaching **Punta Prima**, follow the road to a left-hand bend at the end of the beach. Cross over and walk along CARRER DE XALOC (by the Hotel Xaloc) to the BUS STOP (11; **3h**).

WALK 13: BINIGAUS VALLEY AND COVA DES COLOMS

See also photo on page 97
Distance: 7.6km/4.7mi; 2h
Grade: ● moderate, but with one
short quite strenuous section;
overall ascents/descents of about
125m/400ft; some of the paths
may be overgrown early in the
season, hence the recommendation
below for long trousers and sleeves
Equipment: walking boots
(recommended after rain) or
comfortable footwear, long

trousers, long sleeves, sunhat,
swimwear and towel, suncream,
raingear, picnic (or have lunch at
one of the many restaurants in
Sant Tomàs), plenty of water
How to get there and return:
🚌 or 🚗 to/from Sant Tomàs.
Motorists should park in the car
park at the end of the Me-18 road
from Es Migjorn, near the Es Bruc
restaurant (39° 55.068'N, 4° 2.009'E),
and join the walk at **2**.

A wonderful beach, one of the best hypostyle chambers on
the island, and an unbelievable cave combine to make this
a very enjoyable walk. It starts in Sant Tomàs, a delightful up-
market holiday resort on the south coast.

Begin the walk at the BUS STOP in
Sant Tomàs (🔳). Turn to face the
sea and then turn right, so that you
are walking back the way the bus
has just come and leaving the
resort of Sant Tomàs. At the roundabout at the end of the street turn
left and follow a path on the sea
side of the ES BRUC RESTAURANT,
where you join the CAMÍ DE
CAVALLS (**2**; **5min**).

Keep going in the same direction
along a path above the beach for
12 minutes, at which time you will
be at a large beach at the end of the
Barranc de Binigaus. Make your
way across it towards the BLOCK-
HOUSE shown on page 97, and
turn right along a track. After three
minutes, leaving the Camí de
Cavalls, you will pass through a
gate and find yourself in a small
clearing beside a rather fine WELL
(**3**; **22min**). On your left a locked
gate and 'privado' bar the route
past the Binigaus Nou estate. On
your right a sign indicates the way
to 'COVA DES COLOMS'. You may
spot some faded old red waymarks
here. Follow this narrow path
through bushes and then upwards
in the **Barranc de Binigaus**.

Soon you are walking halfway
up the side of the cliff, along the
edge of terracing. Fifteen minutes
after leaving the little clearing
beside the well, you come to a
CURIOUS CIRCLE OF WALLS, where
the path divides (**4**; **37min**).
Ignore the path to the left for now
(it is your return route): bear right
and go through another gap in a
wall. (An unsigned path which
leads off right here to another
cave, but it's much smaller than the
one you are heading for and a bit
of a scramble to reach.) The main
path soon begins to descend again
to the valley floor.

After another six minutes bear
left, ignoring a path to the right,
and do the same again six minutes
later. A couple of metres further
on, the path forks. Follow the left-
hand waymarked path as it winds
round a bush and climbs slightly
before descending again to the
valley floor. Nine minutes later you
come to a junction with a
CROSSING PATH (**5**; **1h**). Turn right
and start to climb slightly, until
you have crossed the valley and
come to the foot of the opposite
cliff. Here again notices will point

you in the direction of the cave. Zigzag up the side of the cliff until you come to the entrance to the **Cova des Coloms** (**6**; **1h05min**). It is known locally as 'The Cathedral' because of its size!

When you leave the cave, walk to the other side of the valley, back to the junction at the 1h-point of your outgoing route. Turn right to continue in the direction you were previously going. Very soon the path starts to climb quite steeply. After five minutes you pass a small flat area, where there is shade beneath a tree beside a large white rock (pleasant for a picnic). From here the path bears right and begins to climb steeply once more for another five minutes. At the top, follow the path through a gap in a wall, to emerge on a wide track (**7**; **1h18min**).

Turn left and follow this track … or, to extend the walk, see the text opposite.* In about 10 minutes, if you look to your left over the valley, you will see on the opposite cliff-top the two *talayots* of **Sant Agustì Vell**. Just about now you come to a locked gate north of BINIGAUS NOU. This old farm has been converted into a luxury rental property and they don't want people passing by. But it's a pity because one of the island's finest hypostyle chambers lies behind the house. The track becomes ssurfaced here.

A sign points you left, through a gap in the wall and down a side-valley. Back in the **Binigaus Valley**, you rejoin your outgoing route at **4** and retrace your steps to the clearing by the WELL (**3**; **1h40min**). Go through the gate on your right and follow the track to the beach. Turn left, cross the end of the valley, and follow the coast back to the ES BRUC RESTAURANT. Cross the road and re-enter **Sant Tomàs**, then follow the street back to the BUS STOP (**2h**).

*****To extend the walk to Es Migjorn Gran:** Turn right and follow this track. The farm you pass in five minutes is BINIGAUS VELL. Six minutes beyond it, ignore a track to the left, and continue ahead (now on tarmac) through a little hamlet for eight minutes, before reaching the CEMETERY (**8**) at **Es Migjorn**. In a field on your right you will see a fine *talayot*. (*Talyots* are reckoned to be denser in this region than anywhere else on the island.) If you are flagging and don't intend to return to Sant Tomàs, note that there is a BUS STOP (**9**) by the roundabout and sports ground — and your walk will be considerably shorter…

Approaching the talayot *near Es Migjorn (Extension)*

See map opposite; see also photos on pages 2, 11

Walk a: Ermita de Santa Maria (2km/1.4mi; 45min; ● moderate, with an ascent/descent of 155m/500ft on a good track; shaded)

Walk b: La Marcona (6km/3.7mi; 1h30min; ● easy, with an ascent/descent of just 80m/260ft)

Walk c: Ruma Vell (8km/5mi; 2h20min; ● strenuous, with ascents and descents of about 150m, including one steep stretch on concrete)

Equipment: walking boots (Walk a) or comfortable footwear, sunhat, suncream, raingear, binoculars, picnic, plenty of water

How to get there and return: 🚌 or 🚗 to/from Ferreries. Motorists should park just north of the bus stop on Avinguda Dr Franco (39° 59.146′N, 4° 0.811′E)

Approaching Ferreries from the east, you cannot fail to notice the brightly coloured tower of a little chapel perched on top of a hill overlooking the town. Walk a takes you up to that chapel, from where you will have splendid views over the town and surrounding countryside. Walk b may well be the quietest walk you will do — apart from time spent in the cheese factory. Make sure you do it in the morning, when the cheese factory is open. Walk c follows a cycle trail across a crest north of Ferreries, affording splendid views over the northern beaches of Pregonda and Binimel-là, the lighthouse on Cap de Cavallería — and of course to the omnipresent Monte Toro.

Begin Walk a at the BUS STOP/CAR PARK in **Ferreries** (**1**): cross to to the RESTAURANT BAR VIMPI beside the ROUNDABOUT. Walk along the street to the left of the restaurant. It is CARRER DE SON GRANOT, but you will not see the name until you are halfway along it. Cross AVINGUDA DE SON MORERA and the RIVER, and keep straight ahead. At the end of this street, climb a flight of steps. At the top, follow a narrow path to the right; then, after about 20m, turn left on a wider, crossing path. This is an old pilgrims' trail to the little church of St Mary on the hilltop. Look out for the 'stations' — large

View from near the gates to Son Vives farm towards Binimel-là and the lighthouse on Cap de Cavallería; the sign in the lower left-hand corner of the photograph is for cyclists (see 'Cycle routes' panel overleaf)

stones inscribed with the titles of the Virgin Mary. When you meet another crossing path/track (**2**; **4min**) turn right and follow it as it winds up for 15 minutes, to a little gem of a church, the **Ermita de Santa Maria** (**3**; **25min**). Only the tiny sanctuary is completely enclosed, the body of the church has only low walls and no roof. Two stone benches along the rear wall provide the only seating. Behind the church, beyond a small building, there is perhaps the prettiest shady picnic spot on the whole island, with stone table and benches.

Begin your descent now to return to the town. After 15 minutes turn left at **2** and, four minutes later, turn right down the little path that takes you to the flight of steps. Walk straight ahead along CARRER DE SON GRANOT, to the BUS STOP (**45min**).

Start Walk b by walking away from the BUS STOP/CAR PARK (**1**) by the roundabout along the main road in the direction of Es Mercadal. At the next roundabout (after 300m), turn left and walk to the left of the industrial estate (the *Polígon industrial*). Beyond the estate a wide pedestrian pavement on the left takes you under the ring road flyover and before long the wide road turns into a pleasant country lane. After 15 minutes you will arrive at the magnificent HORT SANT PATRICI cheese factory (**4**), with its splendid manor house set in lovely gardens. It is open for visits morning and evening every day except Sunday. There are cheese tastings and a museum.

When you leave the cheese factory, carry on in the same direction for another five minutes, to where the ROAD FORKS (**5**; **25min**). Turn left along the CAMÌ

CYCLE TRAILS

These days Menorca caters brilliantly for cyclists as well as walkers. As of press date there are 21 different way-marked cycle trails, and more are being developed all the time. Especially notable is a trail that crosses the island in six stages (for which there is a pamphlet with general information and sketch maps); it mostly uses country lanes and tracks. Of course there is also the Camí de Cavalls — great fun for the MTB enthusiast, but even so, sometimes you will have to discount and carry the bike.

The Menorca Tourist Board (www.menorca.es) offers very good interactive maps of all their cycling trails — you can see them superimposed on a wide range of maps (including Google Maps and Google Earth) in a variety of sizes — giving you a excellent overview of the terrain. Bicycles — both push bikes and mountain bikes are widely available for hire.

Cycle trails

ROUND (6) and retrace your steps to the fork (5; **1h05min**).

Turn right (or, for a longer walk, turn left and follow the directions for Walk c from its 25min-point) and walk back past the cheese factory and industrial estate. Go under the ring road and when you reach the roundabout on the main road, turn right and return to the BUS STOP (**1h30min**).

To start Walk c follow Walk b as far as the 25min-point (5). Then bear right on the CAMÍ DE SON PERE. Now brace yourself! After about 500m, the tarmac underfoot is replaced by concrete and the road climbs ever more steeply for some 80m/260ft until it reaches a crest by the farmhouse of SON PERE (7). It is not arduous, but quite unpleasant on a hot day (for cyclists as well!). Notice the picture of the saint for which the farm is named over the door: Saint Peter.

The concrete ends here and the road, now tarmac-surfaced, eases, then descends slightly for another 750m until it passes the entrance to the farm of RUMA VELL (8). Now it's just another 500m to a VIEWPOINT (9; **1h10min**) just

DE LA MARCONA. The road undulates through quiet and lovely countryside for 13 minutes, before bringing you to the entrance to LA MARCONA farm, where the tarmac stops. Although the track continues ahead for some distance, you will only be able to continue for a little over 200m, to where it turns right through a gate to a farm building. At that point, TURN

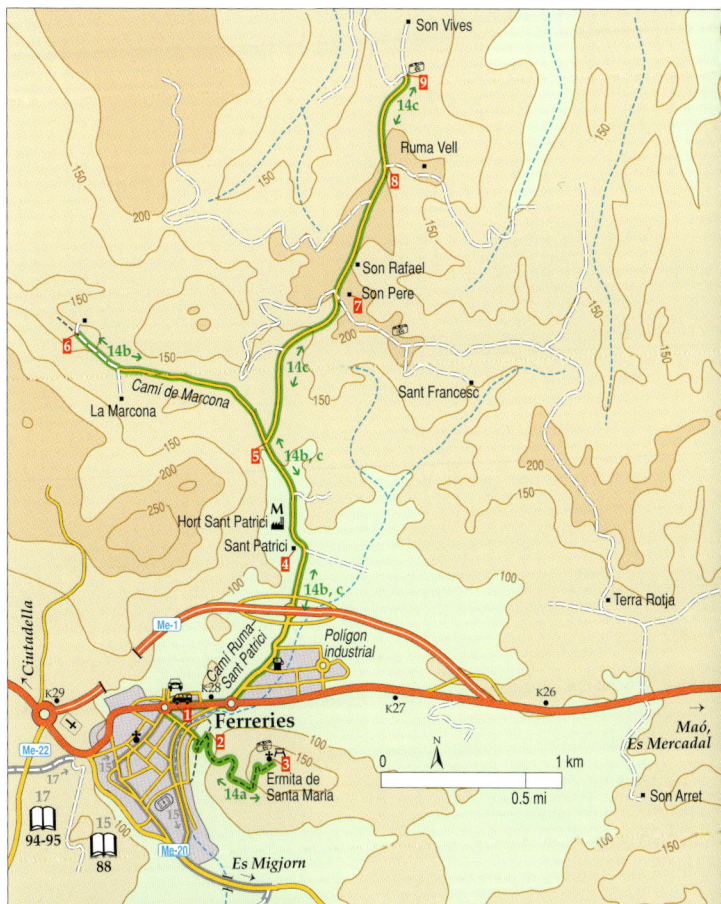

Son Vives

14c

Ruma Vell

8

Son Rafael
Son Pere
7

6 14b

Camí de Marcona
La Marcona

14c

5 14b, c

Sant Francesc

M

Hort Sant Patrici
Sant Patrici
4

14b, c

Me-1

Camí Ruma
Sant Patrici

Polígon
industrial

Terra Rotja

K29

K28

K27

K26

Maó,
Es Mercadal

1 **Ferreries**

2

3

14a Ermita de
Santa Maria

94-95

88

Me-22

Me-20

Es Migjorn

Ciutadella

Son Arret

0   N   1 km

0.5 mi

*Far left: the lovely picnic spot behind
the Ermita de Sana Maria (Walk a);
left: at Hort Sant Patrici (Walks b
and c)*

before the gates of SON VIVES
farm, from where you have the
outlook over the north coast
shown on pages 82-83.

From here retrace your steps
past the CAMÌ DE LA MARCONA
fork (**5**), HORT SANT PATRICI (**4**)
and the ring road. Turn right at the
roundabout on the main road,
back to the BUS STOP (**2h**).

Walk 15: THE GORGES AND PREHISTORIC VILLAGE OF SON MERCER

Distance: 13.3km/8.3mi; 3h35min
Grade: ● strenuous, with an overall ascent/descent of 220m/720ft. No pavement on the Me-20 for some 425m. You will have to climb over the occasional gate, locked to bar the way for cars.
Equipment: walking boots or sturdy shoes, sunhat, raingear, suncream, long trousers, picnic, plenty of water
How to get there and return: 🚌 or 🚗 to/from Ferreries. Motorists should park just north of the bus stop on Avinguda Dr Franco (39° 59.146'N, 4° 0.811'E)
Shorter walks (grade, equipment, access as above)

1   *Barranc de Sa Cova* (10.5km/6.5mi; 2h57min). Follow the main walk to the 1h55min-point at **7**, turn right, and use the notes from the 2h33min-point.

2   *Prehistoric village* (11km/6.8mi; 2h41min). Follow the main walk to the 41min-point at **3** but, instead of turning left, keep straight ahead towards a farm building. Go through a gate and carry on until you reach Son Mercer de Baix (**9**). Cross the farmyard, and in three minutes, when you meet a track coming from the left (**7**), keep straight ahead and pick up the notes at the 1h55min-point.

The farms of Son Mercer are situated on a small plateau entirely surrounded by precipitous cliffs and deep gorges, the *barrancs* of Trebalúger and Sa Cova, and the *torrent* of Son Gras. Such terrain is ideal for bird life. And also for defence. It was here, in one of the most unassailable positions on the island, that a group of talayotic people decided to build their village; the views they enjoyed are breathtaking, as you can see in the photo opposite.

Start the walk at the BUS STOP/ CAR PARK in **Ferreries** (**1**): cross to the RESTAURANT BAR VIMPI beside the ROUNDABOUT. Walk along the street to the left of the restaurant. It is CARRER DE SON GRANOT, but you will not see the name until you are halfway along it. Ahead you will see a hill with a small chapel on top. At the second crossroads, turn right along AVINGUDA DE SON MORERA, with a concrete STORM DRAIN on your left. Follow this tree-lined avenue past the FOOTBALL GROUND and around to the right, to the MAIN ME-20 ROAD; **11min**). Turn left.

After crossing the river bridge, you will have to walk at the side of the Me-20, where there is no pavement. Then turn right at magenta signs for 'Son Mercer de Baix' and 'Poblat'. Go over a cattle grid and climb up the concrete track. In three minutes ignore a track on the left, and in a further 12 minutes, after passing some fine MEGALITHS at the side of the road, you will arrive at the farm of SON MERCER DE DALT (**2**).

Turn right, and then keep straight ahead through a gateway, along a well-made but unsealed road, with farm buildings to your

Left: the Bronze Age settlement at Son Mercer de Baix is the best place on the island to view some of the deep valleys that gouge their way to the sea across southern Menorca. In this photograph the Barranc de Sa Cova leads the eye to Monte Toro (Walk 10) in the distance.

SOME ANCIENT CUSTOMS

Besides telling of their skill with the sling, the writers of antiquity have left us other fascinating glimpses of the inhabitants of prehistoric villages like the one on this walk.

For example, one name for the islands was 'the Gymnasiae', given (according to one writer) 'because the inhabitants go about naked during the summer'. *Plus ça change* … only perhaps we should change 'inhabitants' to 'visitors'. But if that is the case, we must hope that it does not apply equally to another of their customs: 'At the wedding the bride was first possessed by the friends and relations of the bridegroom in exchange for gifts'.

One thing the writers all agree on — the warriors wore no armour in battle. In fact they had little time for metal. There was a ban on the import and use of gold and silver, of which none has been found by archaeologists, and the victorious warrior much preferred to take his spoil in women and wine. In fact they prized women highly, and if their women were carried off by enemies, they would make every effort to ransom them. Lacking gold, they would give three or four men of rank in exchange.

left and a lovely farmhouse on your right. In five minutes, past a slurry pit and another gateway, ignore a track on the right. Then, 100m further on, turn left down a broad track, climbing over a GATE (**3**; **41min**). *(But if you should find 'Privado' signs here — or the farmer has deterred passage with thorny vegetation, keep straight ahead with Shorter walk 2!)* After eight minutes (500m)

This important junction is passed twice during the walk: at 1h55min and at 2h33min. The flat countryside beyond the typical Menorcan wooden gate is deceptive. Between the cowshed and the distant farms deep, steep-sided valleys cut through the landscape. Incidentally, the farms' name illustrates perfectly the multiplicity of Menorquín spellings. There are no less than four versions — Mercé, Marcé, Marcer, Mercer. I have chosen the last because it is on the farm gate.

the track turns right, through a gateway, and narrows. In four minutes go through another gateway; 100m further on, climb over a third iron gate. Ahead is the **Torrent de Son Gras**. Descend now to the valley floor (**4**; **1h08min**).

Pass through a gap in a wall, into a large field. Early in the summer, if it is in crop, walk along the right-hand edge (but watch out for brambles). When the crop has been harvested it is easier. At the end of the field you exit through a gap into a short, walled-in track. Turn left and walk down the track. Turn right at the end and go through a gate on your right into a large cherry ORCHARD. Cross the orchard, walking along the right-hand boundary, and go up steps past an outbuilding. Go through a gate and turn left. Carry on along a good track above and to the right of the orchard at the farm of SON FIDEU (**5**; **1h22min**). If you should ever have trouble leaving the cherry orchard by this gate, carry on walking along the right-hand edge of the field for 100m, where another gate will allow you access to the track.

You now climb back out of the valley, above the **Barranc de Sa Cova**. After some 20 minutes go through a gate (**6**; **1h44min**). Ahead of you, in a field, is a rather splendid *naveta*. All the gateways between this point and the junction at 1h55min are cattle grids with wooden gates beside them. The track turns right at another one in 50m, to cross a wide field. When, in three minutes, you pass another gate, you will see the farm of Son Mercer de Baix ahead. You pass two more gates, in three and eight minutes, and go by the shed seen in the photo at the

left, before coming to an important JUNCTION (**7**; **1h55min**), where the farm is to the right. Turn left on a walled-in track. *(Shorter walk 1 turns right here; Shorter walk 2 comes in here and keeps straight ahead.)*

Just over 1km further on, a large sign announces the PREHISTORIC VILLAGE (**8**; **2h15min**) over to your left, beyond a gate; there is a site plan and information in English and German as well as the two local languages. Most of the buildings are little more than foundations, but there is one hypostyle chamber that is more intact, with three pillars, typically wider at the top than the bottom, supporting the roof. For the best views, walk up to the rear of the village and look out eastwards over the Barranc de Sa Cova (photo on page 86).

When you leave the village, retrace your steps past the track you climbed from the valley (**7**; **2h33min**), and cross the SON MERCER DE BAIX farmyard (**9**). In seven minutes go through a gate, and eight minutes later another. Pass some farm buildings on the left and then the track you took to descend into the valley (**3**; **2h53min**). Go by SON MERCER DE DALT (**2**) and the MEGALITHS, and descend the twisting track back to the MAIN ME-20 ROAD (**3h10min**) at **Ferreries**.

Turn left. Pass your outward route and fork right on CARRER DE MIGJORN GRAN. Pass the FOOTBALL GROUND and fork right to cross the little **Plaça Menorca** and continue along CARRER PAU PONS. This brings you into the main square, the **Plaça Espanya**, where you turn right to follow the AVINGUDA VERGE DEL TORO back to the BUS STOP (**3h35min**).

Walk 16: CALA MITJANA AND TREBALÚGER BAY (WITH OPTIONAL EXTENSIONS TO SANT TOMÀS)

See map on pages 94-95; see also photos on pages 27, 96
Distance: 6.5km/4mi; 2h (add 15min overall if travelling by bus)
Grade: The entire route is very well signed with waymarking posts — at first along the Camí de Cavalls. ● The section between Cala Santa Galdana and Cala Mitjana is easy. ● The section between Cala Mitjana and Trebalúger Bay has some short but quite difficult climbs and descents and requires some agility. It is *not recommended for small children, the elderly or infirm.*
Equipment: walking boots (for the section between Cala Mitjana and Trebalúger Bay) or comfortable footwear, sunhat, raingear, suncream, picnic, plenty of water, swimwear, towel, binoculars
How to get there and return: 🚌 or 🚐 to/from the roundabout at the entrance to Cala Santa Galdana. Then walk or drive towards the 'Mirador de sa Punta'

(the last exit from the round-about). After 600m, the walk starts on the short cul-de-sac road 'Carrer Camí de Cavalls' on the left; park nearby (39° 56.097'N, 3° 57.696E).

Short walk: *Cala Santa Galdana to Cala Mitjana* (5km/3mi; 1h30min; ● easy; equipment as above, but comfortable footwear will suffice). Follow the walk to **3** and return the same way.

Extensions: *to Sant Tomàs by coastal path (a) or Camí de Cavalls (b)*
Walk a: 10km/6.2mi; 2h50min; grade and equipment as main walk *beyond Cala Mitjana:* ● this is strenuous walking — the ups and downs on the whole stretch are around 250m/1000ft). 🚌 to Cala Santa Galdana to start; return by 🚌 from Sant Tomàs. See the map and notes overleaf.
Walk b: 11km/6.8mi; time/access/ ● grade/equipment as Walk a. See the last paragraph on page 92.

P erhaps because it is one of the island's loveliest bays, Cala Trebalúger is one of Menorca's most closely-guarded secrets. As beautiful as the beach is the valley behind it, where the gorges seen on Walk 15 finally meet the sea.

Begin the walk at the INFORMATION BOARD on the CARRER CAMÍ DE CAVALLS (**1**). Beyond the turning circle continue along a short track through a wall. After 20m the path divides. Fork left in the direction of houses and a stone wall. Ten minutes along the path runs through a gateway and takes you to a track. Turn right, and after 150m, turn right again and go through a gateway beside notice boards. Ignoring a path to the right and then two to the left, follow this wide track downhill until you reach the sea at **Cala**

Mitjaneta (**2**; photo on page 27). On your left are more notice boards. These explain the working of a former LIMESTONE QUARRY which lies at the end of a short path to the left.

Continue to follow the track for eight minutes, until you come to steps going down to **Cala Mitjana** (**3**; **25min**; Picnic 10). Behind the *cala* is a large car park with picnic tables. (The Camí de Cavalls — and Extension Walk b above — head off from the northeast corner of the car park, running inland via the Barranc de

MARITIME ZONE MARKERS

From the high water mark for six metres inland, all the coastline of Spain belongs to the state, and along this strip the walker has right of access (unless it has been appropriated by the military). The boundary of this maritime zone is indicated by small concrete markers inscribed 'ZMT'. You will see these markers on all the coastal walks in this book

Photo: Cala Trebalúger

Trebalúger. The *Camí* doesn't come back to the coast until the Platja de Binigaus. *Walkers* may wonder why, since a perfectly well waymarked coastal path (the 'Sender des Litoral' already exists, the *Camí* has been routed inland along this stretch. Probably the answer is that the path from here to Binigaus would not be 'safe for travellers on *horseback*'. But do not be astonished to encounter macho mountain bikers on either of the strenuous extensions described overleaf.)

Head straight across the beach, towards a MARITIME ZONE MARKER similar to the one shown above, and climb onto the limestone ledge. Follow a stepped trail to the top of the cliff. Five minutes should see you at the top, where the path leads you to a drystone wall. Bear slightly left and follow the path into a wood — only before you do so, take time to walk to your right, to a viewpoint overlooking the lovely *cala* you have just left. After walking into the wood for about 100m, ignore a track to the left and keep ahead on the well-worn path. In seven minutes ignore a track on the right, and turn left. Two minutes later fork left, pass a LIMEKILN, and after 15m turn right (**15min**).

The path cuts through two walls, and in four minutes emerges from the wood into a field. Walk beside the bushes on your right to the far side of the field and re-enter woodland. Go through a gap in a wall, and then, slowly at first, begin to descend. The last ten minutes of descent, mostly on cut steps, are quite steep — take care: the drop from the last step down into the narrow river is about 1m/3ft and requires agility. You may have to paddle across the end of the stream to reach the sand of a glorious bay, **Cala Trebalúger** (**4**; **1h05min**).

It is unlikely to be deserted; not

91

only is it visited by boats bringing holidaymakers for a barbecue lunch, but since the opening and waymarking of the through route to Sant Tomàs this hitherto infrequently visited stretch of coast will see many more walkers. But you should find plenty of open space shaded by pine trees, where you can picnic. Before leaving the beach, walk away from the sea and through the wood, to look out over the river at the end of the valley. Not only is the view most attractive but, if you are lucky, you may also see one of Menorca's most attractive birds, the bee-eater, which nests here. If not, you should at least see a heron as some kind of consolation.

If you are walking back to Cala Santa Galdana, retrace your outgoing route back to the INFORMATION BOARD on CARRER CAMÍ DE CAVALLS (**2h**).

Extension a: If you are carrying on to Sant Tomàs along the coast, be prepared for many more ups and downs, but all the potentially vertiginous drops are well protected. There are plenty of waymarker posts. Landfalls en route are **Cala Fustam** (**35min**; this beach could compete with Cala Sa Torreta for seaweed!), **Cala Excorxada** (**55min**), and **Punta Rabiosa** (**1h10min**). Eventually you come to the BLOCKHOUSE shown on page 97 (**1h28min**), where Walk 13 turns up into the **Barranc de Binigaus**. From here it's under 20 minutes' walking — mostly along the beach — to the BUS STOP at **Sant Tomàs** (**1h45min**; **2h50min** from Cala Santa Galdana).

Extension b: You leave the main walk at the **25min**-point. *Barrancs* en route are: **Trebalúger** (**1h**), **Sa Torre** (**1h40min**) and **Binigaus** (**2h10min**), before you reach the BUS STOP at **Sant Tomàs** (**2h30min**; **2h55min** from Cala Santa Galdana). *NB:* If you go to Cala Trebalúger and back before following this extension, add 1h30min — in which case why not go out on the coastal Extension a and return to Cala Santa Galdana on the *Camí?*

Walk 17: CALA SANTA GALDANA • TORRE TRENCADA • CALA MACARELLA • CALA SANTA GALDANA

Distance: 21km/13mi; 5h30min
Grade: ● moderate, with overall ups and downs of about 250m/ 820ft; some gates require agility. Quite a bit is now on tarmac; if this displeases you, try the Shorter or Alternative walk
Equipment: comfortable footwear, sunhat, raingear, suncream, picnic, plenty of water, swimwear, towel
How to get there and return: 🚐 or 🚌 to/from Cala Santa Galdana. By car, take the middle road at the roundabout at the entrance to the resort and turn right over the bridge. Park in the large car park on the right.
Shorter walk: Barranc d'Algendar (6km/3.8mi; 1h20min; ● quite easy, with no appreciable ascents; equipment, access as main walk). Follow the main walk to the 13min-point (**2**). Turn right here, and carry on along the valley floor. After seven minutes, ignore a track to the right crossing the valley and, on coming to a second gate, climb

over the wall at the side of it. Six minutes later, keep to the cart track to make your way through a field. Another 17 minutes' walking will bring you to a wonderful outlook over the Barranc d'Algendar. A fence blocks further progress, so retrace your route to the start.
Alternative walk: Cala Santa Galdana to Ferreries (15km/ 9.3mi; 3h; ● grade, equipment and access by 🚐 as main walk; return on 🚐 from Ferreries). At **4**, the 1h57min-point in the main walk, you join the cycle route between Ciutadella and Ferreries. Follow this to the right. It runs through the gorge of the Algendar *barranc* and comes into Ferreries just north of the junction of the main town road and the Me-20. Although about 3.5km is missing from our map for the latter part of this walk, the route is very well signposted. Pick up the map on page 85 or 88 to check the finish in Ferreries.

W alk up the *barranc* of Algendar while the birds are singing, have a picnic lunch around a megalithic table in a Bronze Age village, enjoy the beauty of Macarella's valley, refresh yourselves on its beach, and finally walk beneath pines back to Cala Santa Galdana.

Start the walk at the BUS STOP/ CAR PARK at **Cala Santa Galdana** (**1**): turn right and walk away from the sea. Walk beside the **Algendar** River into the valley. Beyond a splendid palm tree the metalled road becomes a gravel track. Ten minutes into the walk you reach a gate. Three minutes later the TRACK DIVIDES (**2**; **13min**). Take the rising track on the left. After about 15 minutes you pass the entrance to SON MESTRES farm on the left and in another 25 minutes or so come to

the SANTA GALDANA farm buildings (**3**; **55min**).
Curl right, then left, past the farm, keeping the farmhouse on your right, passing a cowshed on your left, and going beneath power lines. At the end of the farm drive climb a stile over another gate and turn right on a metalled country lane. There will be little traffic because it leads nowhere. In eight minutes, when the lane turns left, you will see on the hill in front the three farms of TORRE PETXINA: Nou, Vell, and Mercadal. As you

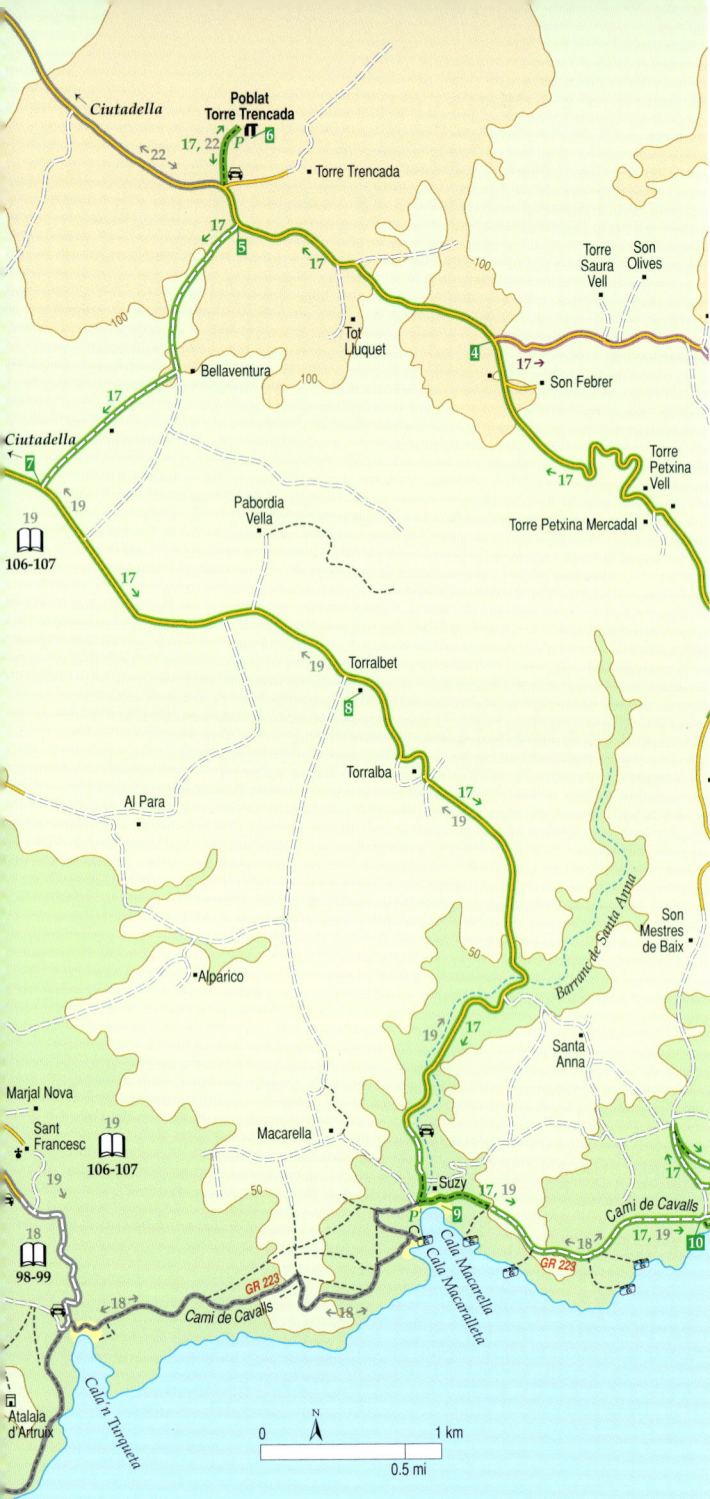

Ciutadella

Poblat Torre Trencada
17, 22 ↑ P
6
■ Torre Trencada

22 ←

17

17 →
5
17 ↖

100

■ Bellaventura
17 ↙
100

■ Tot Lluquet

100

Torre Saura Vell
Son Olives

4
17 →
■ Son Febrer

Ciutadella
←
7
17 ↖

Torre Petxina Vell
← 17

19 ↙

Torre Petxina Mercadal ■

📖 19
106-107

17 ↙

Pabordia Vella

19 ↖

Torralbet
8

Al Para ■

Torralba ■
17 →
19

Barranc de Santa Anna

Son Mestres de Baix

■ Alparico

50

19 ↙   17

Santa Anna

Marjal Nova ■
■ Sant Francesc

📖 19
106-107

Macarella

50

17 ↙

17 →

Suzy
17, 19
9
P

Cami de Cavalls

17, 19 →
10

📖 18
98-99

← 18

GR 223

Cami de Cavalls
← 18

18 →

GR 223
← 18 →

Cala Macarella

Cala Macarelleta

Cala'n Turqueta

🏛 Atalaia d'Artruix

N

0   1 km

0.5 mi

walk up to the farms, the hill to your right is (appropriately enough) Torre Petxina (115m/380ft).

Beyond the farms you cross the **Santa Anna Valley**, and climb to pass Torre Petxina SCHOOL and the entrance to SON FEBRER farm. In four minutes, as you pass under power lines, ignore a road on the right; it's part of the Ciutadella/Ferreries cycle route (**4**; **1h57min**). *(But turn right here for the Alternative walk to Ferreries.)* The main walk follows this cycle route to the left. You will pass the entrance to TOT LLUQUET farm in 13 minutes, and nine minutes later a GATED TRACK on the left (**5**; **2h19min**) — part of the cycle route to Ciutadella. You will be returning along this track after visiting the prehistoric settlement ahead. Two minutes later you will be in the little parking area provided for visitors to the site, from where a signposted path leads across the fields to the prehistoric settlement of **Torre Trencada** (**6**; **2h29min**; Picnic 13).

To continue the walk, return to the car park and turn left. Ignore the road on the left to Torre Trencada farm, and walk straight ahead until you come to the gated track you saw earlier at **5**. The gate requires agility; then turn right along the track. It is barred to motorised traffic — otherwise it would make a handy short cut for cars from the Ferreries/Ciutadella highway to the southern beaches, enabling them to avoid Ciutadella.

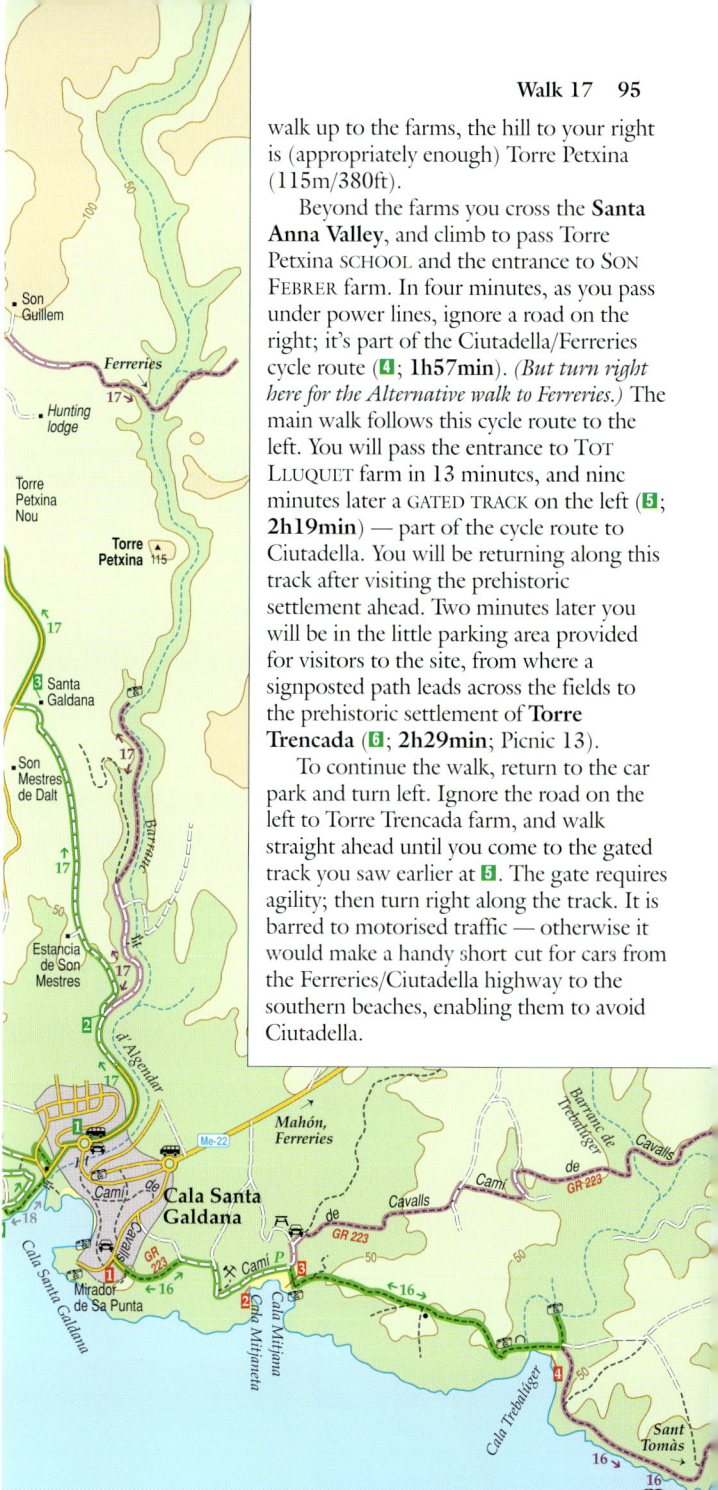

In nine minutes pass farm buildings, and four minutes later follow the track to the right, leaving Bellaventura farm (and the cycle route) to your left. You pass one more house on your left before reaching a tarmac road (**7**; **3h10min**). (Walk 19 follows this road west to Sant Joan de Missa.) Turn left here. Having passed the drives to BELLAVENTURA and PABORDIA VELLA farms, you will come to the farm of TORRALBET (**8**; **3h35min**).

Keep on the road for seven minutes, until the way forks. Take the track to the left signed 'MACARELLA', which bypasses the farm of TORRALBA. Go through a gateway, over a cattle grid, and keep straight ahead. In 10 minutes the road starts to descend quite steeply into the valley. It is wooded and shaded now. A little over half an hour past Torralba farm you arrive at **Cala Macarella** (**9**; **4h20min**; Picnic 11; Walks 18 and 19). You will be grateful now for CAFETERIA SUZY, with toilets and showers (open from late April to October).

To continue, join the well-waymarked CAMÍ DE CAVALLS and begin the steep ascent of a splendid wooden staircase with no fewer than 214 steps. Bear left at the top along a wide path. After about 15 minutes the route turns sharply left. Clamber down over rocks, keeping beside a wall on your left as you have done since the path reached the top of the cliff. Two

Cala Santa Galdana: Menorcans regard it as their most beautiful beach and bitterly regret its 'urbanización'. There is no saint named Galdana; the name is a corruption of the Moorish 'Guad-al-Ana' (barranc of St Anne'), after whom the adjacent farm is named.

minutes later do something similar (you may spot waymarks here).

During the next eight minutes ignore occasional paths to the right, and continue to follow the wide track beside the wall (shown in the photo below). You will come to a wall with two gaps in it. Choose the HIGHER GAP (**10**; **4h50min**), on the left. Go through it: this gives access to a good track. Walk through a pine wood for seven minutes (past a short-cut path) until you come to a T-junction where you turn right. In six minutes turn right at a junction, and six minutes later you will pass through a gate.

Now **Cala Santa Galdana** lies before you (**5h10min**). Turn left and follow the road round to the right. Almost at once go down steps on your right, and go down to the bay past the HOTEL AUDAX. Turn left once more, and walk round the bay to the CAR PARK/BUS STOP (**5h30min**).

Autumn crocuses on the track from Cala Santa Galdana to Cala Macarella

BLOCKHOUSES

Every beach on Menorca where enemy forces could possibly land is guarded with tiny blockhouses of varying dates. Some date from the 18th century, when France and Britain fought over the island, for at that time Maó harbour was Britain's equivalent of America's Pearl Harbour.

These blockhouses have a dozen or so small apertures for musketeers/ riflemen, and are built of stone.

Others date from the Spanish Civil War (1936-9); the small, concrete structures with only one or two openings are machine-gun posts. Some are almost intact, sometimes providing accommodation for bats, others have crumbled away, whilst a few, like so many other ancient buildings here, provide free holiday homes.

Blockhouse at Binigaus (Walk 13)

Walk 18: A COASTAL WALK BETWEEN CALA'N BOSCH AND CALA SANTA GALDANA

Map begins below and continues on pages 100-101; see also photo on page 96
Important note: Since this walk was first published, the Camí de Cavalls has been rerouted *several* times, and we expect the changes to be ongoing. If you find that the situation on the ground differs from our text, *follow the waymarks!*
Distance/time, How to get there and return: See below and page 102
Grade: ● moderate, with ascents/descents of about 200m/650ft overall; on sometimes stony paths or sand; very little shade

Equipment: comfortable footwear, sunhat, raingear, suncream, picnic, plenty of water, swimwear, towel
Shorter walk: Son Saura — Cala'n Turqueta — Son Saura (6.5km/4mi; 1h50min; grade: ● easy; equipment as above) 🚗: See Picnic 20 on page 19 to drive to Son Saura beach. Then pick up the Cala'n Bosch to Cala Santa Galdana walk below at **5** and follow it as far as Cala'n Turqueta (**7**). Then turn to the 1h36min-point of the Cala Santa Galdana to Cala'n Bosch walk at **7** (page 104) and retrace your steps back to Platja de Son Saura.

S ometimes winding through beautiful countryside, sometimes beside the sea, continually descending to breathtaking beaches, often following ancient tracks and passing
ancient buildings, this walk — which follows the Camí de
Cavalls throughout, may well prove to be your favourite. It is
described fully in both directions. Since it is a long walk, you
may wish to follow only part of it and then retrace your steps.
(To make this easier, at each time check I have inserted, *in italics,*
the time check if walking in the reverse direction.)

From Cala'n Bosch to Cala Santa Galdana

Distance: 16km/10mi; 4h22min
How to get there: 🚌 to Cala'n Bosch (alight at the Platja Cala'n Bosch bus stop). Or 🚗 (only if you intend to walk part way, and retrace steps to Cala'n Bosch).

Drive to Cala'n Bosch. At the roundabout take the third exit and keep following 'Son Xoriguer' on the road circling the resort. Then, by the Carema Beach Hotel (on your left), keep straight on for 200m to park by the bus shelter on the right (39° 55.630'N, 3° 50.163'E).

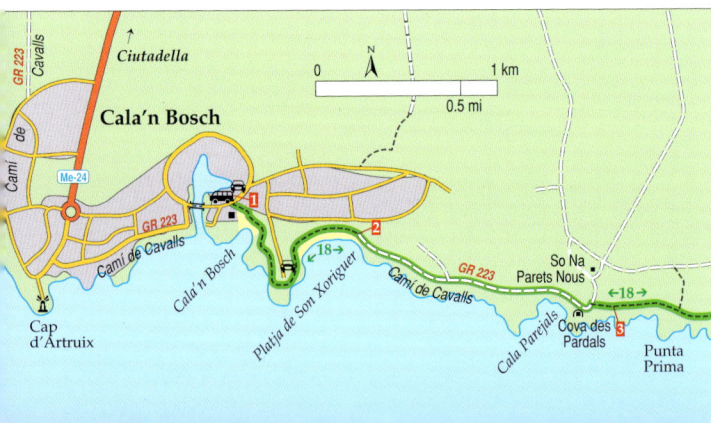

To return: 🚌 from Cala Santa Galdana or 🚐 from Cala'n Bosch

Begin the walk at the BUS STOP/ CAR PARKING in **Cala'n Bosch** (**1**): take the lane opposite the shelter (with red/white waymarks of the Camí de Cavalls on a pole), then follow the boardwalk behind the beach, climbing up to the headland on the far side. Walk round the headland on a well-trodden path and you will arrive at the adjacent bay, **Son Xoriguer**. Carry on until you are nearly at the opposite HEADLAND (**2**; **20min**) *(4h07min)*, from where the *Camí* takes a sandy track going away to the left. Soon you are skirting a drystone wall. The sea is never far away to your right, as the way takes you between bushes. After 500m a similar track goes off left, but ignore that, and continue to walk parallel with the sea.

In 100m you will come to a wall that goes down to the coast. Go through a gateway and shortly you will reach **Cala Parejals**. I find this a forbidding place, much eroded by the sea and giving the impression that the whole cliff is about to collapse. It is watched over by a MACHINE GUN EMPLACE- MENT, the first of many military buildings and blockhouses along this coast. Notice the steps by a little white building which lead to

a mooring in a cave (the COVA DES PARDALS) below. The building houses the machinery for raising a boat out of the water. Beyond this building fork right; the left fork leads to So Na Parets Nous farm. After 200m go through a WOODEN GATE (**3**; **45min**) *(3h42min)*.

Continue with a wall to your left and **Punta Prima** to your right. In six minutes go through a gap in a wall, ignore a path to the left, and walk across rocky ground towards bushes opposite. The *Camí* winds round the next seaweedy bay, **Cala de Son Vell**. It turns right behind the cove and leads through bushes to a wall going down to the sea, where you go through a GATEWAY in the wall (**4**; **1h01min**) *(3h22min)*. (An ancient cart track comes in from behind you to the left here — once it was part of the *Camí*. Its bedrock surface is deeply worn and rutted in places, testifying both to its antiquity and the volume of traffic which once made its way to this isolated bay in an age when the sea offered the easiest way of moving about the island.)

Beyond the gateway, follow the path ahead, veering towards the sea. In a couple of minutes you pass between a pair of CAVES. The one on the right is worth exploring, since it is a good example of a Menorcan troglodyte

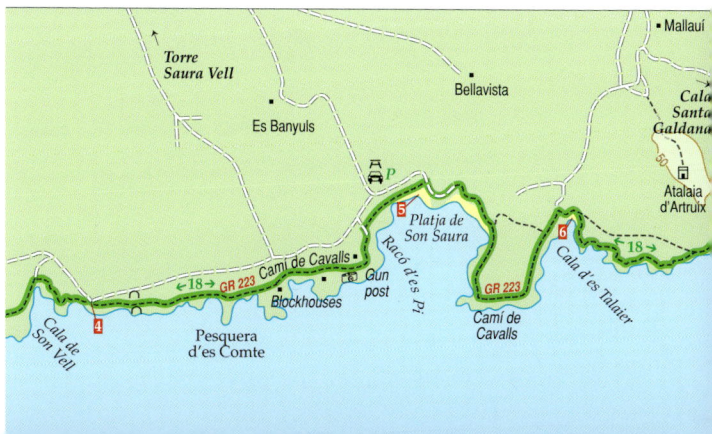

home. The central pillar giving support to the roof, and the pilaster on the right, are common features.

The path continues eastwards until reaching shrubby terrain. Pass between bushes on the left and the **Pesquera d'es Comte** on the seaward side. Cross the end of a headland, beyond which is a little *cala*. Continue round the beach, past two BLOCKHOUSES. In 200m you will arrive at the **Racó d'es Pi**, with the beach of Son Saura in view. If you look straight across the bay, you will see another military post on a hilltop — the medieval WATCHTOWER OF **Artruix**, shown on page 105. The path descends to sea level, crossing a slipway and passing another GUN POST. Here you join another ancient cart track. When you come to a wall, go through a gate and walk onto the beach of **Platja de Son Saura** (**5**; **1h40min**) (*2h37min*). (*This is the starting- and end-point for the Shorter walk.*)

Walk round the first half of the bay, then cross the little rock outcrop that bisects the bay. Follow the path to a bridge over a drain and walk round the second half of the bay. Some 200m before the end of the bay, ignore the path to the left, crossing the headland. Follow the *Camí* along the cliffs and through a GATEWAY in a wall. Rise up, then turn right down to

Cala d'es Talaier, just about perfect for your picnic (**6**; **2h**) (*2h21min*). The *Camí* rounds the *cala* on a track before descending a path on the right at a SIGNBOARD. Over to your left you will see the **Atalaia d'Artruix**.

Referring now to the map below, after 10 minutes turn right along a narrow path. This brings you close to the sea, with lovely views. Keep following the waymarked path towards Turqueta Beach, going through a wall at **Punta des Tambors**, below the watchtower. It's not long before you're on the beach of **Cala'n Turqueta** (**7**; **2h44min**) (*1h36min*). (*The Shorter walk returns from here.*)

From here follow the unmissable *Camí* uphill and through a gateway in a wall. Then keep straight ahead, with a wall on your left. After another seven minutes the path brings you to a MAJOR JUNCTION, where you turn right (**8**; **3h06min**) (*1h13min*). Shortly, ignore two adjacent paths on the right, and descend through a small valley that bring you to another superb little beach, **Cala Macarelleta** (**9**; **3h16min**) (*56min*).

Cross to the left-hand side of the beach (as you face the sea), then take the steps cut into the rock, which turn left and wind their way up to the top of the cliff.

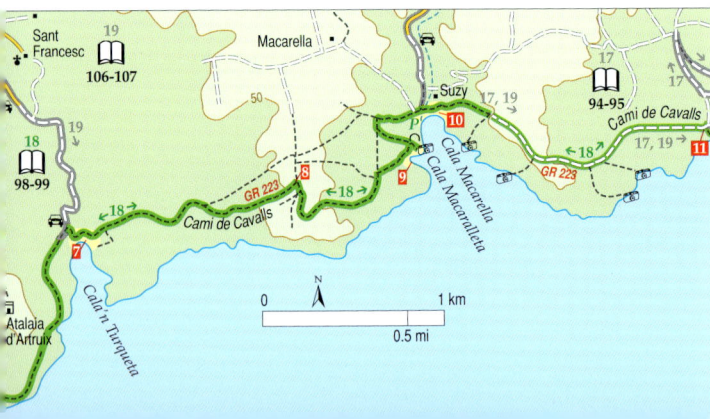

Cala Macarelleta

From the top of the steps a short path leads to a T-junction with a broad path. Your way is left, but before leaving, walk in the opposite direction to the END OF THE HEADLAND, where you have splendid views over both Macarelleta beach and its larger neighbour, Macarella. This is arguably one of the best viewpoints on the trail.

Retrace your steps and pass the short path. Two minutes later, when the path turns right, ignore a

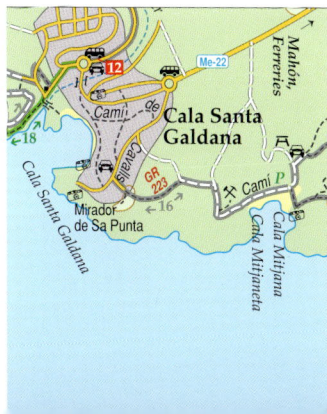

path on the left, and in 50m turn right down a rocky path. Go through a gap in a wall, and keep descending until you emerge at the rear of **Cala Macarella** (🔟 ; **3h34min**) *(40min)*. Walk across the beach, setting for Picnic 11 (and also visited in Walks 17 and 19). On the opposite side is a fine beach bar and restaurant, the CAFETERIA SUZY (open from late April to October). The café also provides toilets and shower. To continue the walk, begin the steep ascent of the splendid wooden staircase shown overleaf — with no fewer than 214 steps. Bear left at the top along a track.

Skirting a wall on your left, you pass four paths on the right to viewpoints over the coast and sea. Continue to follow the wide track beside the wall (photo on page 97). Eventually you will come to a crossing wall. There are two gaps in it. Go down to the lower one (**11**; **4h07min**) *(15min)*. Ignore the track to the left (used in Walk 17), and follow the stony path down the side of the cliff towards **Cala Santa Galdana**. Soon you will pass the end of a footbridge and go down steps to the road beside the HOTEL AUDAX. Follow the road beside the river towards a large car park just beyond the roundabout. The BUS STOP is next to the CAR PARK (**12**; **4h22min**).

No fewer than 214 steps of an imposing wooden staircase take you down to Cala Macarella when you're walking from Cala Galdana — or you climb them when walking east from from Cala'n Bosch.

Cala Santa Galdana to Cala'n Bosch

Distance: 16km/10mi; 4h32min
How to get there: 🚌 to Cala Santa Galdana. Or 🚗 (only possible if you intend to walk part way and then retrace your steps to Cala Santa Galdana). Drive to Cala Santa Galdana. At the roundabout as you enter the resort, take the middle road down into the town and turn right over the bridge. Park in the large car park on the right.
To return: 🚌 from Cala'n Bosch or 🚗 from Cala Santa Galdana

Leaving the BUS STOP OR CAR PARK in **Cala Santa Galdana** (**12**), turn

left, and **begin** by walking towards the sea, keeping to the right of the river (map on pages 100-101). Ahead of you, beyond the HOTEL AUDAX, steps take you to the base of the cliff and to a footpath which climbs past the end of a footbridge and up the side of the cliff in the setting shown on page 96. In five minutes go through a gap in a wall (🔟; **15min**) *(4h07min)*, and very shortly turn left along a wide track. For the next 12 minutes you will skirt to the left of the drystone wall.

The good CAMÍ DE CAVALLS waymarking will prove helpful to you at critical moments for the whole of this walk. But for the moment, on this most popular stretch of the *Camí*, the way is clear — a wide, pine-shaded walking trail at the left of a wall, where you ignore four paths on the left heading seawards to signposted viewpoints. Some 10 minutes (600m) after the wall on your right ends, you descend the 214 steps of the imposing wooden staircase shown opposite to **Cala Macarella**, the setting for Picnic 11 and also visited on Walks 17 and 19. You pass the end of the garden of a fine beach bar and restaurant, CAFETERIA SUZY, open from late April to October (🔟; **40min**) *(3h34min)*.

Cross the beach and go over the water drain. You will meet a number of similar water courses, which prevent the ends of the *barrancs* forming marshes. To your left you will notice, halfway up the cliff face and overlooking the sea, a couple of CAVES and the wide ledge that leads to them — doubtless highly desirable residences in Menorca's troglodytic period. To your right, at the foot of the cliff, is a track leading to the

as his head, and he has an orangey-red breast and a bright white collar. He loves to perch on some spike rising above the bush, and is not too timid, so that he will often sit there 'chatting' while you get a good look at him.

Crows are rare, but one that you will see is the raven, usually alone.

The following are also quite common: greenfinches and sereins (both green), alpine swifts (as well as ordinary and pallid swifts), corn buntings, short-toed and thekla larks, grey and purple herons, kestrels, linnets, crag martins, house martins, swallows, spotted flycatchers, red-legged partridges, tawny pipits (like wagtails, only brown), house sparrows, nightingales, whinchats, rock pigeons, turtle doves.

There are several waders and ducks that you may see in the bays and lagoons, especially at S'Albufera. Cormorants are common.

I have left the best two until last. One is quite a large bird, glorious pink in colour, with a splendid crest and wings that look like a piano keyboard when it flies past. It is the hoopoe. I have met them on many of my walks, usually in pairs, and always with the same thrill of excitement. The other is the bee-eater, described on page 44. *The place to see and learn about the island's bird life is the Albufera Natural Park at Es Grau (Walk 2).*

As for the rest of the fauna, there are snails and lizards everywhere, especially in the drystone walls. Black beetles, butterflies and bees abound. But the really exotic creature which will delight children is the tortoise, often seen on woodland paths.

Macarella estate (closed to walkers). Straight ahead is a Camí de Cavalls signpost for Cala en Turqueta, and a wide path.

Walk up this path away from Macarella Beach, and pass through a gap in a wall. Carry on ahead, until you reach a T-junction. Here turn left and, 50m further on, fork left. Follow this path to the END OF THE HEADLAND (about 200m), for the views you get over two *calas,* Macarella and Macarelleta — some people consider these the finest views on the whole walk.

Then retrace your steps for 100m and turn left along the narrow waymarked path. The path goes straight to the edge of the cliff, where a stone staircase has been cut from the rock. It is edged in part by traditional wooden fencing. Descend now to **Cala Macarelleta**, the little gem of a beach shown on page 101 (**9**; **56min**) *(3h16min)*. Part of the beach has been roped off to protect the fragile ecosystem.

If you can bear to leave Cala Macarelleta, walk to the left of the back of the beach, and up a wide path along the side of a small valley. Ignore a path on the right. After ten minutes' further walking there is a section of eroded track that has been repaired with concrete, and just beyond it ignore a turning to the left. A minute later, turn left along the well-trodden path (**8**; **1h13min**) *(3h06min)*. Two buildings can be seen ahead: the medieval WATCH-TOWER OF **Artruix**, and the cream-coloured Mallauí farmhouse. Nine minutes later the path goes through a gate in a wall, and in five minutes forks. Turn right along the wider path, descend through woodland, and finally emerge on the beach of **Cala'n Turqueta** (**7**;

1h36min) *(2h44min)*. *(The Shorter walk returns here.)*

To continue the walk, go past the seaward end of the car park and climb a few steps. The *Camí* now shadows a wall up a wooded slope, with no views. Now referring to the map on pages 98-99, go through a gate in another wall. There are some short but steep and rocky sections now, with ups and downs to take you round the mouth of the 'turquoise' bay.

The wide path goes through a wall at **Punta des Tambors** below the watchtower and heads on to the next bay, where you reach a signpost. Turn left here, on a wide path that rises and falls as it circles to a mapboard above **Cala d'es Talaier** (**6**; **2h21min**) *(2h)*.

Climb past the mapboard, then turn left at a signpost (in front of two walls). Go through a gateway, then ignore a wide path on your right cutting across the headland; follow the *Camí* round the cliffs until you emerge at **Platja de Son Saura** (**5**; **2h37min**) *(1h40min)*. This large but shallow beach is one of the most beautiful on the coast. It is the setting for Picnic 20 and the starting- and finishing-point for the Shorter walk.

When you are ready to leave Son Saura beach, walk round the edge towards the rock outcrop on the far side, and cross another marsh-draining water course. Turn left and follow the path over the rock outcrop to the second half of the beach. Walk round that until you come to a wall, go through the gate and take the path to the left. You round the coast to a GUN POST and continue just above the sea to the next bay, which is guarded at both ends by BLOCKHOUSES. Then make your way across the rocky headland and on between a shrubby area on your right and the sea on your left. As you continue westwards across this rocky terrain you will pass between a pair of CAVES. The one on the left is rather nice, with a pilaster and central pillar. Two minutes beyond the caves, go through a GATEWAY (**4**; **3h22min**) *(1h01min)*.

Beyond the gateway the *Camí* forks left, to continue beside the sea. This is another example of how the route has been changed over the years, to develop safe paths ever closer to the coast: when first surveyed, the path used the ancient cart track running inland from the gateway. The trail now rounds the **Cala de Son Vell**, a rocky inlet, and continues with a wall to your right and **Punta Prima** to your left. Some six minutes (400m) after meeting the wall, you go through a WOODEN GATE (**3**; **3h42min**) *(45min)*.

Shortly, you pass a small white building. Steps beside it lead to a mooring in a cave below (the COVA DES PARDALS). The building houses the machinery for raising a boat out of the water. Walk next round **Cala Parejals**, where the cliffs are steadily crumbling into the sea. Pass a gun emplacement and go through another gateway, to walk parallel with the sea for 100m. Then ignore a track to the right, and for another 500m walk between bushes with the sea on your left, to arrive at the beach of **Son Xoriguer** (**2**; **4h07min**) *(20min)*. Round the beach and then the headland. This will bring you to the final beach, at **Cala'n Bosch**. On the far side stands the Cala'n Bosch Hotel. Walk past it to the BUS STOP in front of the hotel entrance (**1**; **4h32min**).

WATCHTOWERS

All the coastal walks in the book will take you past at least one watchtower. Some of them date back as early as the 16th century and were built to try to avert future disasters on the scale of the Turkish assaults of 1535 (see page 33) and 1558 (see page 113). Others were built by the British or French during the wars of the 18th century, while yet more were built by the British during the Napoleonic War at the beginning of the 19th century.

The tiny, cylindrical towers you will come across from time to time are the remains of windmills. Some have been partially restored and turned to other uses, like those seen on page 25 at Sant Lluís (Walk 12) and page 113 at Ciutadella (Walk 20).

Photograph: the Atalaia d'Artruix (Walks 18 and 19)

Walk 19: ES PUJOL DE SON TICA AND CALA MACARELLA

Distance: 17.5km/10.8mi; 4h35min

Grade: ● moderate, on account of the length, with ups/downs of about 200m/650ft; mostly on country roads (watch for motorists making for the beach!), with a short stretch along the coast

Equipment: comfortable footwear, sunhat, raingear, suncream, picnic, plenty of water, swimwear, towel

How to get there and return: 🚗 only accessible by car or taxi. Driving to Ciutadella from the Maó direction, turn left at the round-about as you reach the town (signs for the beaches of Macarella and Turqueta). Park on the left after 5km at Sant Joan de Missa (39° 58.100'N, 3° 52.883'E).

Shorter walk: Sant Joan de Missa — Cala Macarella — Cala Santa Galdana (11km/6.8mi; 3h10min). ● Grade, equipment as main walk. Access: 🚌 taxi from Ciutadella to the Ermita de Sant Joan de Missa. Follow the main walk to **8**. Then turn to page 101 and follow Walk 18 from **10** to the end (map pages 100-101). Return by 🚌 from Cala Santa Galdana to Ciutadella (via Ferreries).

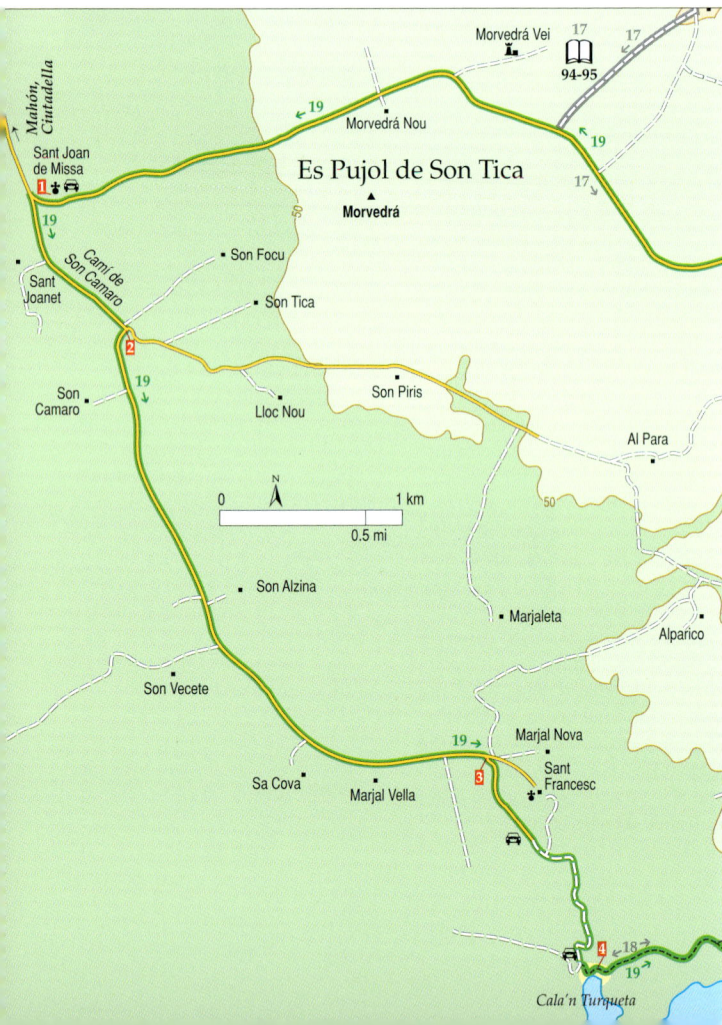

This walk starts at the picturesque country church (*ermita*) of Sant Joan de Missa (St John the Baptist). This *ermita* seems to have been built shortly after the Reconquest of Menorca from the Moors by Alfonso III in 1287 and occupies an important place in local folklore. The walk circles a region known as Es Pujol de Son Tica and visits three lovely beaches.

To begin, leave **Sant Joan de Missa** (**1**) and turn right (west), walking back to the T-junction. At the junction, turn left along the CAMI DE SON CAMARO. In **10min** you pass the entrance to the farm of SON FOCU on the left and immediately come to a T-JUNCTION (**2**). Take the road to the *right* (our original route, the quieter lane to the left, is now closed to walkers beyond the farm of Al Para). In just over 4km keep right at a fork for 'Cala en Turqueta' (**3**; where

MARJAL NOVA and SANT FRANCESC are to the left). Under 500m further on you come to a first, large parking area for the beach. Keep downhill on the metalled lane through woodland to pretty **Cala'n Turqueta** (**4**; **1h25min**).

From the beach, walk past the toilets at the seaward end of the lower car park and bear left to climb up a sandy path, the CAMÍ DE CAVALLS. For a few minutes you rise through a pine wood, before emerging into more open country. Now the path bends left; ignore a path on the right. The path winds through low bushes to a wall, where you pass through a gateway. Keep straight ahead now, with a wall on your left.

After another seven minutes the path has widened and brought you to a MAJOR JUNCTION, where you turn right (**5**; **1h48min**). Ignoring two adjacent paths off to the right, descend through a small valley that bring you to the superb little beach shown on page 101, **Cala Macarelleta** (**6**; **1h58min**).

Cross to the left-hand side of the beach (as you face the sea), then take the steps cut into the rock, which turn left and wind their way up to the top of the cliff. From the top of the steps a short path leads to a T-junction with a broad path. Your way is left, but before leaving, walk in the opposite direction to the END OF THE HEADLAND, where there is a splendid VIEWPOINT (**7**) over both Macarelleta beach and its larger

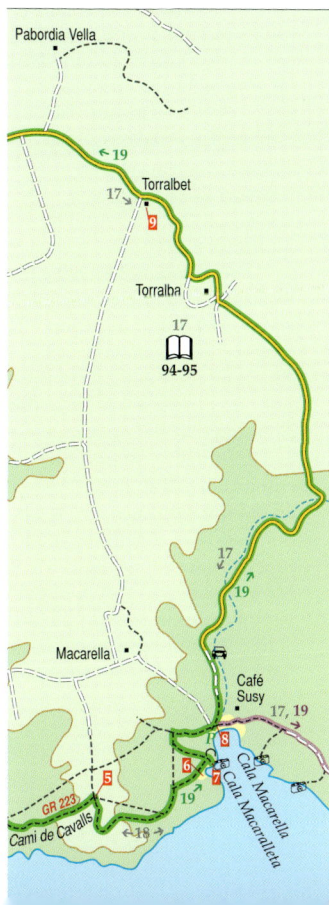

CHAPELS

Outside the island's small towns there are few villages. There are however several small churches dotted about the countryside at central locations to which farming families can come for mass. They are known as *ermitas* ('hermitages'). Walk 19 begins at the *ermita* shown above. Walk 1 passes another *ermita* dedicated to St John the Baptist, Walk 9 that of Sant Llorenç (St Laurence), and Walk 14 that of Santa Maria (Saint Mary).

In the past even these churches were too difficult for some families to get to. Sometimes it was easier to bring the priest to the family, and occasionally you will notice a chapel built next to a remote farmhouse, as at Binissaida on Walk 6.

Finally, Walks 7, 8 and 11 take you to what remains of two churches built in the very early days of Christianity, at Es Fornàs (page 60) and Son Bou (page 76).

Photo: Sant Joan de Missa. Every year the people of Ciutadella celebrate the birthday of St John the Baptist on 24 June with splendid displays of horsemanship in which more than 100 riders take part. The ceremonies begin on the eve of the festival, with all the horsemen riding out to this church to sing the evening service.

neighbour, Macarella. Many think this is one of the best views on the south coast.

Retrace your steps and pass the short path. Two minutes later, when the path turns right, ignore a path on the left, and in 50m/yds turn right down a rocky path. Go through a gap in a wall and descend to emerge at the rear of **Cala Macarella** (**8**; **2h15min**; Picnic 11), also visited on Walks 17 and 18. From late April to October you will find sustenance (as well as toilets and shower) at CAFETERIA SUZY.

Walk to the rear of the beach and go through the CAR PARK. Continue along the lane as it makes its way up the beautiful **Barranc de Santa Anna**, spoiled only by the many cars that now use it since it has been metalled to the car park. After 20 minutes pass on your right the entrance to SANTA ANNA farm, and 25 minutes later make your way past TORRALBA farm on your left. After a further 20 minutes you will reach TORRALBET farm (**9**; **3h20min**).

Keep ahead to pass the gate to PABORDIA VELLA on the right after another 10 minutes. Beyond here the pine woods on your left decline, and the road dips to the right, to cross a low valley. After climbing out, the road bends left and eventually you pass the entrance to MORVEDRA VEI (**4h**), an old fortified farm (see the panel on page 125). Again the road turns left, soon passing MORVEDRA NOU, a rural hotel/restaurant. It is all downhill now, and in 25 minutes you are back at **Sant Joan de Missa (4h35min)**.

Walk 20: A WALKABOUT TOUR OF CIUTADELLA

See town plan overleaf

Distance: 5km/3mi for those travelling by bus; 7km/4.3mi with the extension to the Castell de San Nicolau; under 7km/4.3mi if you arrive by car; about 3h

Grade: ● easy, but with some steps

Equipment: comfortable shoes of any sort, sunhat, raingear, suncream

How to get there and return: 🚌 or 🚐 to/from Ciutadella. 🚗: Approaching Ciutadella along the Me-1, turn left at the horse roundabout shown on page 25. There is a car park to your left (40° 0.193'N, 3° 51.008'E). Walk back to the horse roundabout, turn left and follow the Camí de Maó to the Plaça d'Alfons III. I find this by far the most convenient place to park, but it adds just under 1km each way to the walk. There is also car parking in the Plaça d'es Born (if you arrive early enough), in which case start the tour at **4**. Visitors coming in from the beaches on the Torres 🚐 should start at the Plaça de S'Esplanada/Senplaxada (**9**). Those arriving on the TMSA 🚐 from the Maó direction alight in the Plaça de la Pau (**10**): referring to the town plan, make your way from there to the junction of Negrete and Purissima to begin (see page 114).

T he dismantling of the city walls was begun in 1868, so that 'the Citadel of Menorca' could expand. Their line is marked by a series of wide avenues which divide the old city from the modern part. Our walk lies mostly within the confines of the old city, which is where the most impressive and important buildings are to be found. Care must be taken to follow the route exactly as described, for it meanders through the maze of narrow streets which give Ciutadella its very special character, wherein aristocrat and artisan live side by side.

The walk begins in the **Plaça d'Alfons III** (**1**). This square is named after King Alfonso III of Aragon, nicknamed 'the Liberal', the hero of the Reconquest. Before 1868 the gate to the old city stood on this spot. To left and right, where there are wide avenues today, the massive city walls rose up. Here Alfonso entered Ciutadella in triumph, and every 22 January that event is celebrated. A statue of St Anthony Abad (on whose feast five days earlier the Moors had been vanquished) is carried in a cortège led by three horsemen. One of them bangs on the ground three times with his staff at the entrance to the city, to announce the King's arrival.

On the opposite side of the square from the Camí de Maó is the CARRER DE MAÓ. This is the beginning of the main street through the town. Before starting along it, turn round and look back at the corner of the Camí de Maó, where the WINDMILL shown on page 113 has been turned into a popular bar. One of the chief attractions of Ciutadella is apparent as you walk between the houses which frame the entrance to Carrer de Maó — its many elegant buildings.

Some pleasant shops are to be found in Carrer de Maó, before it opens out into the delightful **Plaça Nova**. Walk along the left-hand side of the square, and continue into the narrow SES VOLTES (also called J M Quadrado), bordered

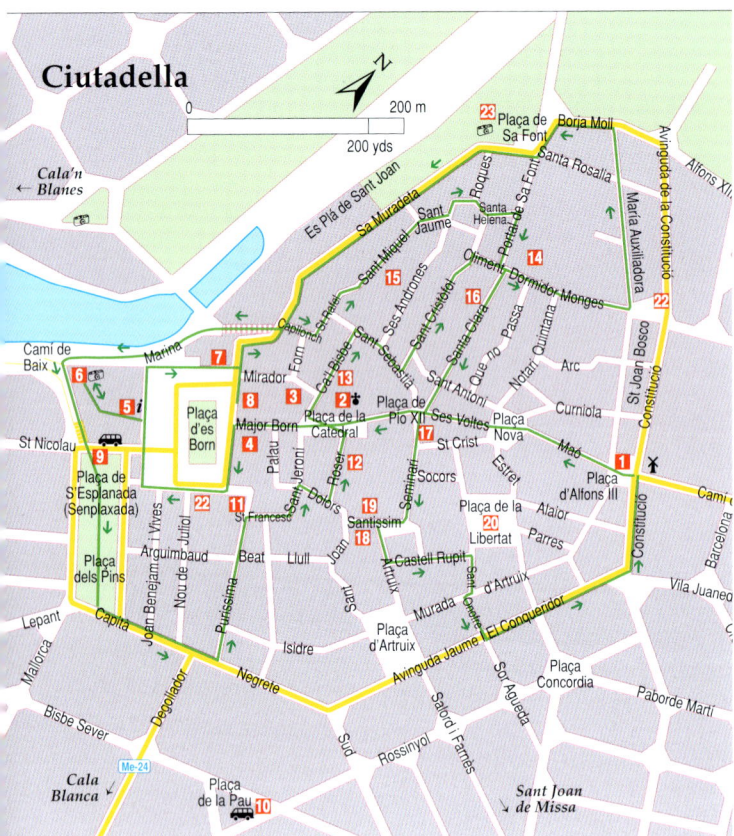

Ciutadella

0   200 m
200 yds

Cala'n
← Blanes

Plaça de
Sa Font   Borja Moll

Santa Rosalia

Es Pla de Sant Joan

Sa Muradeta

Sant Miquel
Jaume

Santa
Helena

Sant Andrones

Sant Cristòbal

Oliment Dormidor Monges

Camí de
Baix

Marina

Capllonch

From

Mirador

Sant Sebastià

Ses Andrones

Santa Clara

Quc Pça

Nctar Quintana

Arc

Curniola

St Nicolau

Plaça
d'es
Born

Major Born

Plaça de la
Catedral

Plaça de
Pío XII

Sant Antoni

Ses Voltes

Plaça
Nova

Maó

Sant Jeroni

Palau

Besen

St Crist

Estel

Plaça de
S'Esplanada
(Senplaxada)

Plaça de
S'Esplanada

Socors

Plaça
d'Alfons III

Camí

Plaça
dels Pins

Arguimbaud

St Francesc

Sant Dolors

Santíssim

Plaça de la
Libertat

Alalor

Parres

Barcelona

Joan Benejam i Vives

Julfiol

Nou de Juliol

Beat

Llull

Sant Joan

Castell Rupit

Artruix

Purísima

Sant Oliver

Murada

d'Artruix

El Conqueridor

Vila Juanea

Lepant

Capità

Mallorca

Degollador

Sud

Negrete

Plaça
d'Artruix

Isidre

Avinguda Jaume El Conqueridor

Sor Agueda

Plaça
Concordia

Paborde Martí

Bisbe Sever

Me-24

Cala
Blanca

Plaça
de la Pau

Salord i Farnes

Rossinyol

Sant Joan
↓ de Missa

on each side with arcades. These arches *(voltes)* are a feature of Ciutadella. At the end of Ses Voltes you come to **Plaça de Pío XII**.

Carry on in the same direction into **Plaça de la Catedral**, passing **St Mary's Cathedral** (**2**) on your right. This was where the Moors built their principal mosque. As soon as Alfonso expelled them, the mosque was consecrated as a Christian church, as were all other mosques on the island. Gradually a new Christian church was built to replace it, being completed in 1362. All that remains today of the Moorish building is part of the minaret, which was incorporated

into the tower on the north side. The church is enclosed within a windowless curtain wall, which may be part of the original building or may have been added after the Turkish destruction to provide extra defence. So damaged was the building at that time that restoration took 150 years. The contrasting west entrance is a neo-classical addition dating from 1813. The interior suffered badly from vandalism at the hands of the Republicans during the Civil War.

From the square keep going in the same westerly direction past the Olivar Palace along CARRER MAJOR DEL BORN, which leads

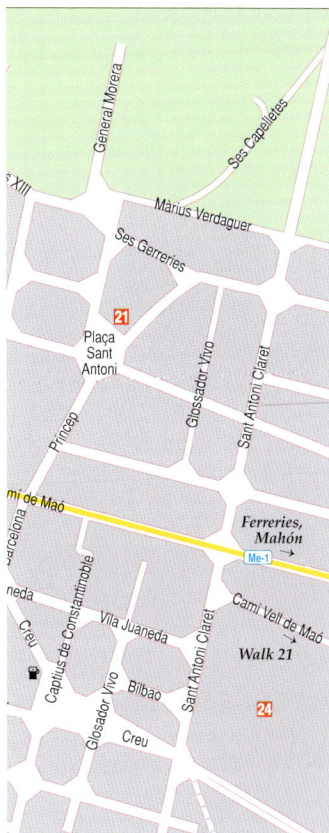

CIUTADELLA — KEY

1 Plaça d'Alfons III and windmill
2 St Mary's Cathedral (Santa María)
3 Olivar Palace
4 Salort Palace
5 Ajuntament (Town Hall) with Tourist Information Office
6 Bastió des Governador
7 Teatro Borne
8 Torre-Saura Palace
9 Torres Buses (from the beaches)
10 TMSA Buses (from Maó)
11 Sant Francesc (St Francis) Church
12 Nuestra Señora del Rosario Church
13 Bishop's Palace
14 Santa Clara Convent
15 San Miguel Church
16 Lluriach Palace
17 Santo Cristo Church
18 Saura Palace
19 Martorell Palace
20 Market
21 Hospital
22 Post Office
23 Bastió de Sa Font
24 Old Municipal Cemetery

into one of the finest city squares in the whole of Spain: the **Plaça d'es Born**. Dominating the square, a great obelisk commemorates the brave resistance put up by the townspeople to the Turkish attack. The Latin inscription (by Josep María Quadrado) translates 'Here we fought until death for our religion and our country in the year 1558'.

Turn left on leaving Major del Born and pass on the corner one of the most impressive mansions in Ciutadella, the **Salort Palace** (**4**). In summer, it is often open to

Obelisk in Born Square

visitors between 10am and 2pm (the entrance is back the way you came, about 30m/yds to the right along Major del Born, through an open, unmarked, wooden door, directly opposite the larger, more imposing entrance to the Torre Saura Palace). Remember to look up: here in Menorca the principal reception rooms are always on the first floor. The great wooden doors at ground level usually open on to spacious courtyards.

Continue your walk round the square until you reach the building opposite, the **Ajuntament** or town hall (**5**), which also houses the Tourist Information Office. To the left of the building a passage leads to steps up to a 17th-century tower known as the **Bastió d'es Governador** (**6**), from where you have a splendid view over the harbour. Note that it is only open in the morning. The town hall was once the governor's palace. The present building is the result of a 19th-century restoration. Its crenellation and round arches, and the palm trees in front, give this corner of Ciutadella a deliberately Moorish appearance: it was here that the Alcazar, the palace of the Kaid, stood for 385 years. Do go inside. Much can be seen, even during working hours. There is a Gothic reception hall with panelled ceiling and wrought-iron lamps, a small museum which contains the battle banner of King Alfonso, and portraits of the city's notable citizens of yesteryear (as well as one of King George III, which the British left behind, and another of the American admiral, David Farragut). After working hours, from 6-8pm (12-1pm on Saturdays) more of the rooms can be viewed. In the mayor's office is the 'Llibre Vermell', the medieval

'Red Book', recording the privileges King Alfonso gave to the island.

Facing you across Born Square now, to the left of Carrer Major del Born is the most splendid of all the houses in Ciutadella — the palace of the Count of Torre-Saura. The family coat-of-arms is emblazoned above the doorway. As you walk along the north side of the square you will see below you what little remains of the medieval fortifications and the lovely harbour. Just before the corner you pass the theatre, the **Teatro Borne** (**7**). Turn left after you have finished inspecting the **Torre-Saura Palace** (**8**) and leave the square by Carrer de sa Muradeta, which first turns right and then left to bring you to the top of a wide flight of steps that take you down to the harbour.

At the bottom turn left and walk along the quayside beneath the great walls, and maybe stop at one of the cafés for refreshment. Then continue alongside the harbour and turn left up Carrer de Marina behind the town hall. Where the street turns left, you will see a flight of steps ahead. Go up these steps. (But first, I recommend a half-hour's diversion of about 2km: Turn sharply right here and follow the Camí de Baix above the *cala* as far as the 16th-century **Castell de Sant Nicolau** and bust of Admiral Farragut, mentioned on page 115. This detour is not shown on our plan.)

Then return to this point either along Camí de Baix or go down steps by the harbour lights and walk along the landing stage. Cross Camí de Sant Nicolau to the park opposite, the **Plaça de S'Esplanada** (or **Plaça de Senplaxada**). This is where the

ABOUT THE CITY

As far as the British were concerned, Menorca was an appendage to Port Mahón. Most other rulers of the island preferred the harbour of Ciutadella. Although by no means so deep nor so long as that of Mahón, the port of Ciutadella was adequate for the shallow draught shipping of former times, and it had the advantage of being nearer both to Mallorca and mainland Spain. So it was here that the largest fortified city of the island grew up, hence its name 'Citadel'.

The history of the city begins in the time of the Carthaginians, who knew it as Iamno. In 123 BC, Quintus Caecilius Metellus was sent by the Senate of Rome to suppress the Balearic pirates, which was sufficient excuse for him to add the islands to the Roman Empire (and reward himself by taking the title 'Balearicus'). Ciutadella changed its name slightly to Iamona, and 140km (85mi) of roads were built across Menorca to link it with other Roman forts at Santa Agueda and Mahón. The first Islamic raid occurred as early as 707, when Moorish pirates came in search of slaves, but the conquest of Menorca was delayed for two more centuries, until it was added to the Emirate of Cordova in 902. The Kaid, as the Muslim governor was called, chose Ciutadella to be his capital. He built his palace, the Alcazar, overlooking the harbour. For nearly four centuries the Moors knew the city by the Arabic name of Medina Minurka — 'The City of Menorca', and here they built their chief mosque. At the Reconquest in 1287 Alfonso III of Aragon entered Ciutadella on 22 January and declared it the island's capital. Throughout the remainder

Northeast corner of Born Square (top) and the windmill/ bar on the Camí de Maó

of the Middle Ages there was continual rivalry between Ciutadella and Mahón, as the latter grew steadily in importance.

The most momentous event in Ciutadella's history took place in the year 1558, when 150 Turkish ships under the command of Barbarossa's successor Piali, carrying 15,000 troops, sailed into the port. After nine days' siege the city fell. Its 3495 inhabitants, including the governor Don Bartolome Arguimbau, were taken as slaves to Constantinople, and the city was sacked so completely that when a new governor came out, he was compelled to spend his first night in a cave — there were no houses left standing in Ciutadella.

But the city was rebuilt, and many of the captives were ransomed and returned home. However, even before the coming of the British in 1708, the governor moved his residence to Mahón, which served to intensify the rivalry between the two cities.

The harbour; below: St Mary's cathedral

that continue the line of the former walls. The first one is AVINGUDA DEL CAPITA NEGRETE, and here you turn left. Captain Negrete had the misfortune to be the senior army officer in Ciutadella on the day the Turks sailed into the harbour (see 'About the city', page 113). He had under him 40 soldiers whom he had brought from Castille to repair the city's defences. Local territorials brought the number of armed men up to about 620.

Pass two streets, Carrer Joan Benejam i Vives, and Carrer Nou de Juliol, and turn left along the third, CARRER PURISSIMA. This leads back to Born Square where, on the corner with the Plaça d'es Born, is the **Church of Sant Francesc** (**11**). Architecturally the church is a mixture of 14th-century Gothic that survived the destruction and restoration baroque. When James II of Mallorca succeeded Alfonso in 1291 (he was only 23 when he died) he appointed a Royal Commission to organise Menorcan affairs which met in this church.

Just before the end of Carrer Purissima, opposite the church, turn right along CARRER DE SANT FRANCESC (San Francisco). At the end, turn left along CARRER DE SANT JERONI. This street is bordered on the right by one of the older mansions, that of the Sintas family. At the junction with CARRER DE NOSTRA SENYORA DELS DOLORS turn right and pass (on the left) the Plazuela del Rosario. Turn left along the next street, CARRER ROSER: on the right is a visual treat, the gorgeous little church of **Nuestra Señora del Rosario** (**12**), from which the

TORRES BUS STOPS (**9**) are situated. Visitors who have come in on TMSA BUSES from Maó had best make their way here from the **Plaça de la Pau** (**10**).

Walk away from the bus stops the length of the tree-filled park, leaving the Born Square and its obelisk behind you. This is where the first section of the walls once stood. At the end of the park you are at the beginning of the avenues street gets its name. (This church too was vandalised during the Civil War.) It was begun at the end of the 17th century by the Dominican friars. When the British came in 1708 they requisitioned it and held Church of England services there for the benefit of the British soldiers. The extravagant baroque decoration of the main doorway is, like the Chapel of the Immaculate Conception in Maó's St Francis Church (see page 37), decidedly churrigueresque. It now hosts exhibitions.

As you make your way to the end of Carrer Roser, you will see the Gothic south door of St Mary's Cathedral facing you. On reaching the **Plaça de la Catedral** once more, cross to the far left-hand corner where, opposite the west entrance to the cathedral, No 8 is the home of the Olives family. This mansion was built early in the 17th century. It contains much fine furniture, some made in the 18th century by Menorcan craftsmen from English pattern books, and some French from the time of the brief French occupation of the island (1756-63). Also French is the frieze featuring birds, animals and fishes which runs round the top of the walls in the three large state rooms.

Turn right and continue along CARRER DEL CA'L BISBE, passing on your right the **Bishop's Palace** (13). Christianity arrived early in Menorca, and there was a bishopric here until 484, when the last bishop, Makarius, sailed for North Africa to defend his faith before the heretical Vandal king, Hunnericus, never to be heard of again. Not until 1795 did the Vatican restore its bishop to Menorca and, as had been the case

in the past, he chose Ciutadella to be the seat of his diocese. Previously his palace had been an Augustinian convent.

Facing the end of the street is yet another fine house, the Squella mansion, home of the Marqués de Menas Albas. It was here that the American Admiral David Farragut slept when he visited Ciutadella in December 1867. The bedroom and bed he used are still preserved. Farragut may well be unknown to English readers, but to Americans he is as important as Nelson. It was during the American Civil War that he made a name for himself, by sinking eleven Confederate warships and capturing New Orleans. He was put in command of all the naval forces and created First Admiral of the US Navy in 1866. The admiral's father was born in Ciutadella and had emigrated to the States when he was seventeen. During a goodwill visit of the American fleet to Maó harbour, Admiral Farragut took the opportunity to visit his father's birthplace. Ciutadella took him to its heart. He was fêted and made an honorary citizen. There is a bust of him by the harbour mouth, near the Esmeralda Hotel.

Turn right at the junction, into CARRER SANT SEBASTIA. Pass Carrer de ses Andrones on the left, and turn along the next street on the left, CARRER SANT CRISTOFOL. Then take the second street on the right, CARRER CLIMENT, go under the arch and carry on in the same direction along CARRER DEL DORMIDOR DE LES MONGES (Padre Federico Pareja). On the left is the **Santa Clara Convent** (14), founded through the generosity of Alfonso the Liberal in 1287. Destroyed by the Turks, the convent was rebuilt in the 17th

Fountain in Plaça d'es Born

century. To finance this, the order imitated a practice initiated by Fr Miguel Subirats, the Prior of the Augustinians, to restore his convent (now the Bishop's Palace). They secured from the King of Spain the privilege of offering deeds of nobility to members of wealthy families in return for contributions. Many of the noble families whose houses you see on the walk acquired their titles in this way. The convent was restored once more in 1945. In 1987, on the 700th anniversary of its foundation, a plaque was put up recording its history.

Turn left along CARRER DE MARIA AUXILIADORA, passing the sanctuary of the Salesian Fathers and, at the end, turn left along AVINGUDA DE FRANCESC DE BORJA MOLL and follow the line of the last section of wall to the **Plaça de Sa Font** or 'Fountain Square'. Here you can see the only section of wall still remaining other than by the harbour.

Walk across the square and go along CARRER DE SA MURADETA to the left of the tower that is home to the municipal museum and was once the reservoir for the city's water supply. The ground

Ses Voltes

falls away steeply on your right, giving a view of small terraced gardens on both slopes of the valley. The wide sandy expanse below is **Es Plá de Sant Joan** (St John the Baptist). Notice how the steps lead down through all the gardens to terraces or platforms beside the wall which look out over Es Plá. That is where Menorca's most prestigious festival takes place annually on June 24th, the feast of St John the Baptist. The ceremony goes back to the Middle Ages. It begins with a cavalcade of over a hundred richly caparisoned horses, their riders (*caixers*) in traditional costume. The cavalcade is led by a man bearing the flag of the Knights of St John of Malta. There follow displays of horsemanship, with prancing steeds, and young men doing their best to make them unseat their riders, all to the accompaniment of pipes and tambourines and general merriment. Then these terraces will be thronged with onlookers getting the best — and safest — view of the proceedings. It is the spirit of this festival that is expressed in the statue seen on page 25.

Towards the end of Carrer de Sa Muradeta, immediately before the steps going down to the port, turn left into CARRER DE PERE CAPLLONCH. Ignore Carrer des Forn on the right, and turn left again into CARRER SANT RAFEL. Now is the time to let your imagination have free rein. If ever there were streets which allowed you to pass back through time, they are these alleyways. But do remember that though the layout of the streets may be medieval, or even Moorish, the houses themselves cannot predate 1558. All had to be rebuilt after the Turkish destruction.

Pass on the right the junction with Carrer Sant Sebastià, and follow the street as it turns first right, then left, into CARRER SANT MIQUEL. On the right you will pass **San Miguel Church** (**15**). At the end of the street turn right into CARRER DE SANT JAUME and, almost at once, go left at the junction with CARRER DE SANT BARTOMEU. Turn sharply right at the next junction. After 25m/yds turn left into tiny CARRER DE SANTA HELENA.

Turn right at the T-junction along PORTAL DE SA FONT. Very soon you pass the convent of Santa Clara again, on your left. In the 18th century the convent was the scene of a scandal straight from the pages of a 'Mills and Boon'. The saintly sisters ran a school for young ladies. With the ingenuity of young ladies the world over, three of the pupils managed both to make the acquaintance of, and to fall in love with, a trio of young English army officers. With determined recklessness, the girls fled the convent and hid with the lieutenants, rejecting all attempts to persuade them to return. The Roman Catholic church was up in arms. The girls must be returned to the convent. The governor, General Blakeney, showing a remarkable broadness of mind, refused to force them back against their will. All were duly wed and, I suppose, lived happily ever after.

Keep going in the same direction and enter CARRER DE SANTA CLARA. On your right, No 29 is one of the oldest and most prestigious of the stately homes — **Lluriach Palace** (**16**), home of the Barons of Lluriach, the oldest of the Menorcan titles. Its facade shows that stern rejection of ostentation characterising so many Spanish buildings. It is impressive nonetheless.

At the end of Carrer Santa Clara cross over Ses Voltes (Carrer J M Quadrado) and go along CARRER D'ES SEMINARI. There are three fine buildings here, all on your left. The first is **Santo Cristo Church** (**17**), a tiny baroque gem, built in 1667 and restored in 1967. Outside are classical columns and capitals and an octagonal stone dome surmounted by a stone

A traditional butcher's shop in the market by Plaça de la Libertat

lantern. Within there is a tiny gallery. Lower down the street is a bank which is housed in one of the town's former mansions — a mansion with a story. The British first came to Menorca because of their involvement in the War of the Spanish Succession. King Carlos II of Spain had died childless, and there were two young claimants to the throne, descended from his sisters. One was French, Prince Philip of Anjou, the other Austrian, the Archduke Charles. Inevitably Britain was determined that it could not be the Frenchman. In the war that ensued, the Royal Navy was hampered by having to return to England every winter, and General James Stanhope saw the value to Britain in having the use of Maó harbour. He gained the support of the pro-Austrian party on Menorca, whose leader was Juán Miguel Saura y Morell. In revenge the pro-French party burned his home to the ground. After Stanhope had conquered the island, he had a splendid new house built in Ciutadella for Saura — the one occupied today by the bank. The third building is another church towards the end of the street, now the diocesan museum.

Turn right at the end of Carrer d'es Seminari into CARRER SANTISSIM. Halfway along pass a street on the left (Artruix), which you will eventually follow. But before doing so, walk to the end of the street and look at the building on your left. Now partly an antique shop, it is **Saura Palace** (18), built towards the end of the 17th century. It is finely

proportioned, with beautiful neo-classical decorations round the full-length windows on the first floor. Inside is a broad staircase made in 1718, and the reception rooms are lit by magnificent chandeliers made in La Granja, near Madrid. On the other side of Carrer Santissim is **Martorell Palace** (19), home of the Marqués de Albranca. Like Lluriach Palace, its façade is reserved in decoration, exhibiting again that Spanish architectural puritanism.

Return now to the street you passed earlier, and turn along CARRER DEL PORTAL D'ARTRUIX. Shortly, take the first turning on the left, CARRER CASTELL RUPIT. After some 80m you reach the **Plaça de la Libertat**, diagonally left, built in 1868 and today home to the MARKET (20), sadly in decline since the arrival of super-markets. At the end of Carrer Castell Rupit turn right along CARRER SANT ONOFRE and, after crossing one street, you will come to the AVINGUDA JAUME I EL CONQUERIDOR. 'Conqueror' is the title bestowed on King James I of Aragon for the reconquest of Catalonia and Mallorca. He began the reconquest of Menorca which his grandson Alfonso completed. He did not actually invade the smaller island, but terrified its Moorish rulers into becoming his vassals.

Turn left along Conqueridor and bear left into AVINGUDA DE LA CONSTITUCIO for some 200m/yds, back to **Plaça d'Alfons III** (about **3h**). Those who started at 4, 9 or 10 should now turn back to 1 on page 112 and continue from there.

Walk 21: ALONG THE CAMÍ VELL

See also town plan on pages 110-111 and photos with Walk 20
Distance: 14.4km/9mi; 4h05min
Grade: ● easy; on country lanes and short paths; ups and downs of 100m/330ft overall
Equipment: comfortable footwear, sunhat, suncream, raingear, picnic, torch, binoculars, plenty of water
How to get there and return: 🚌 or 🚐 to/from Ciutadella (alight at the 'Piscina' stop if coming from Maó. 🚌: Approaching Ciutadella along the Me-1, turn left at the horse roundabout shown on page 25. There is a car park to your left (40° 0.193'N, 3° 51.008'E). Turn right on the Camí Vell from the car park.

Shorter and Alternative walks
1 Torre Trencada (7.6km/4.7mi; 2h; ● easy; access and equipment as main walk). Follow the main walk to **5**, then call a taxi to return to Ciutadella. Or take a taxi to start and do the walk in reverse.
2 Ciutadella to Ferreries (17km/10.5mi; 5-6h; ● moderate, with ascents of 250m/820ft and descents of 200m/650ft overall). Access by 🚐 to Ciutadella; return by 🚐 from Ferreries. Follow the walk to **5**, then pick up Walk 17 at **6** on page 95 to walk to Ferreries via the Barranc d'Algendar.
3 Ciutadella to Cala Galdana (19km/11.8mi; 5-6h; ● moderate, with ascents/descents of about 150m/500ft overall). Access by 🚐 to Ciutadella; return by 🚐 from Cala Galdana. Follow the walk to **5**, then pick up Walk 17 at **6** on page 95 and follow it to the end..
4 Ciutadella—Torre Trencada — Naveta d'es Tudons (13.5km/8.4mi; 3h30min; access, equipment and ● grade as main walk, *but you will encounter traffic!*). Follow the main walk to **5**, then return to **4** and follow that narrow country road for 1km to the Me-1. Turn left on the main road for 1km, to the Naveta d'es Tudons (**3**) and, after your visit, call a taxi to return to Ciutadella.

The focus of this walk was originally the cyclopean building shown opposite, but it is no longer accessible from the Camí Vell. If you haven't visited by car or tour coach, you may wish to tackle Alternative walk 4. Inside there is a vestibule and two chambers, one above the other, both of which were used for burials. Unfortunately it is no longer possible to venture inside the *naveta* because in 2018 vandals painted the walls with graffiti (which have been removed).

But the lane leading past the field with the *naveta*, the Camí Vell de Maó, is a joy in itself, and you *will* have access to the *poblat* of Torre Trencada. This lane is also a cycle route, and any of the walks above could be done by cycle, if you're so inclined. *Warning!* This ramble may prove expensive, with paid entry to the quarries, the *naveta* … and a stop to buy cheese!

If you come on the TSMA bus from the Maó direction, or if you drive, you are well placed for the start of the walk. If, however, you come on one of the Torres buses, refer to the plan on pages 110-111 to reach the start of the walk.

Begin the walk along the CAMÍ VELL DE MAÓ, just in front of the electricity substation (**1**) and head east. This lane was first built by the Romans and continued to be used until Sir Richard Kane built the new road in the 18th centur. Cross

the next major road on one of the zebras. Then pass the new CEMETERY — and look out for three *talayots* in a field on your left. You then walk below the RC-2 ring road, continue along the lane through a region of QUARRIES.

Some are still being worked, some have been put to a variety of other uses. The most interesting of these are the S'Hostal Quarries (**2** ; **Pedreres de S'Hostal**), which have been adopted by a group of enthusiasts known as 'Líthica'. The older quarries have been transformed into a botanical garden, while the 20th-century ones are preserved as an example of a working quarry, and occasionally used as an open-air theatre. It's certainly worth a visit to this unusual attraction, as you would see from their website, www. lithica.es. Year round (except January 1-21) they are open from 09.30 to 14.30; in summer there is also an afternoon opening. (Picnic 10 is set in a similar old quarry, close to Alaior.)

Further along the road you will pass the place where the contents of the bins into which you have carefully separated your refuse are taken to be recycled. Another 25 minutes walking will bring you within sight of the massive old farmhouse of ES TUDONS (**55min**). You will notice a (locked) gate and cattle grid on the left; this used to give access to the **Naveta d'es Tudons** (**3**), which you can see over to your left.

Continue along the lane for 20 minutes, to a road junction, where the CAVALLERIA VELLA farm on the right at sells cheese ('Formatges Binigarba'). The road to the left, the CAMÍ BINIGARBA (**4**), brings local traffic from the Me-1, so the Camí Vell will be a little busier

THE NAVETA D'ES TUDONS

The most celebrated cyclopean building on Menorca is the large burial chamber shown above. Various claims have been made for it, including that it is the oldest roofed building in Spain, or indeed Europe. It is certainly a very interesting edifice, in that it contains two storeys and has been extensively restored.

In the 1950s the *naveta* was in a lamentable condition and in danger of total destruction. It was overgrown with bushes, and one end was broken open. Its present splendid state is due to the enthusiasm of two people.

One was Luís Pericot García, Professor of Archaeology at the University of Barcelona, who conceived and masterminded the restoration. The other was María Luisa Serra Belabre, then Director of Maó Museum, to whom the work was entrusted. She was aided by an architect named Victor Tolor.

A grant from the March Foundation made the work possible, and the restoration of the *naveta* was undertaken in 1959/60. Inside there is a vestibule and two chambers, one above the other, both of which were used for burials.

During the excavations María Serra found hundreds of human bones, from at least a hundred bodies, lying on a bed of pebbles. Bronze bracelets still encircled some of the arm bones. Other bronze items and simple jewellery buried with the corpses were also found.

121

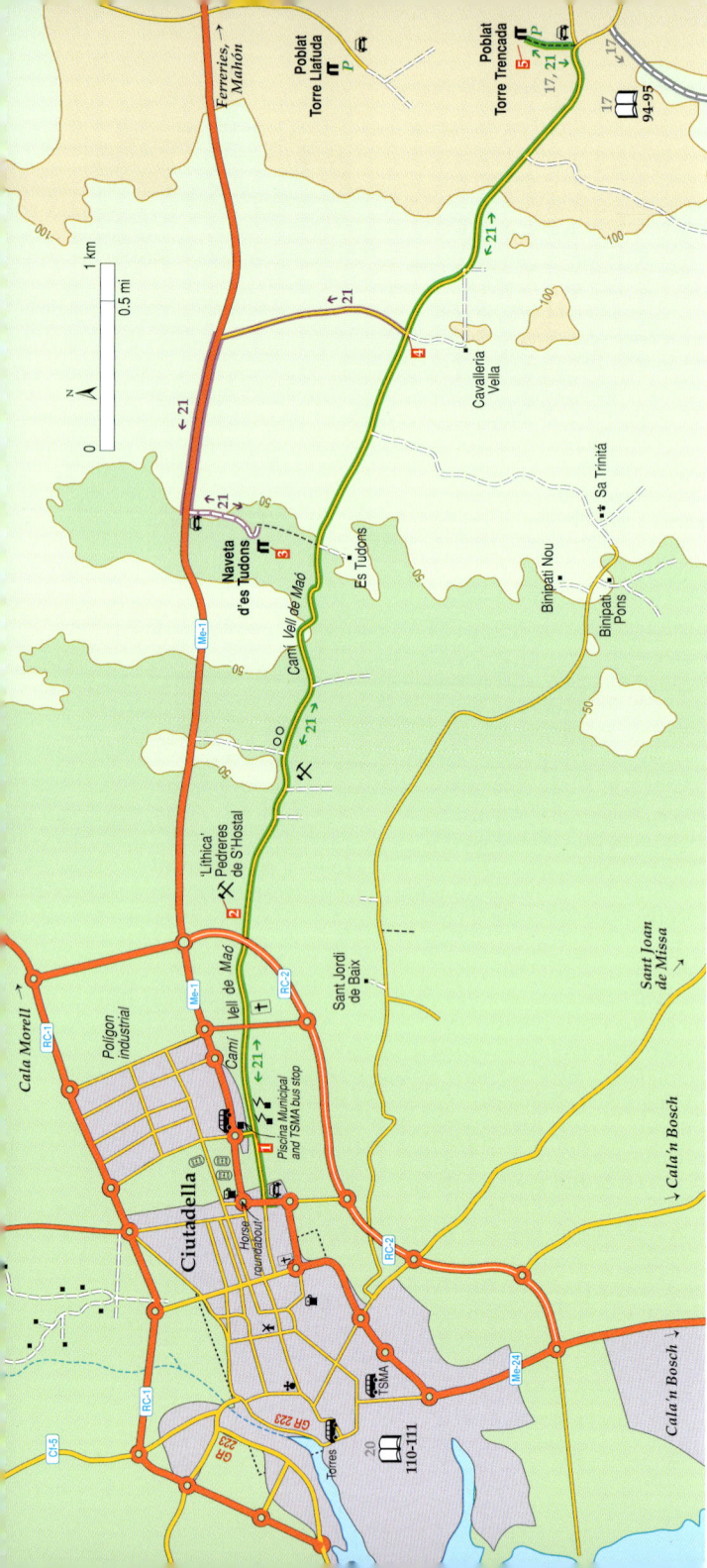

Ferreries, Mahón →

Poblat
Torre Llafuda
π P

Poblat
Torre Trencada
π P
17, 21 → 5 ↙ P
17 ↗
17
94-95

← 21

21 ↗

← 21
⊡
Cavalleria
Vella

1 km
0.5 mi
N
0

← 21
π 3
Naveta
d'es Tudons

Camí Vell de Maó

Es Tudons

Sa Trinità
✝

Binipati Nou

Binipati
Pons

← 21 →

✕
∞

'Lithica'
Pedreres
de S'Hostal 2

Me-1

Me-1

Camí Vell de Maó RC-2

Sant Jordi
de Baix

Sant Joan
de Missa

Cala Morell

Polígon
industrial

RC-1

Camí ← 21 →
1 Piscina Municipal
and TSMA bus stop

Ciutadella

Horse
roundabout

RC-2

Cala'n Bosch

Cala'n Bosch →

RC-1

Cl-5

GR 223

GR 223

Torres

TSMA

Me-24

20 110-111

Cala'n Bosch

Cattle sheds

Cattle shed north of the Me-1, opposite the naveta *at Es Tudons (Walk 21)*

now, but not too busy. The Binigarda lane is the one used in Alternative walk 4; although it is hemmed in by walls, it's certainly wide enough for walkers to get out of the way of any light local traffic.

Under half an hour's walking from here should see you at the car park for the *poblat,* or prehistoric village, of **Torre Trencada**. It is another eight minutes' walking along a signposted path before you come to the site, also visited on Walk 17 (**5** ; **2h**; Picnic 13).

Make your way back to the car park and turn right. Retrace your steps now along the country lane, passing the farm of CAVALLERIA VELLA after 25 minutes. Five minutes later you will lose the traffic returning to the Me-1, and the lane will be a bit quieter. In 25 minutes you will be back passing the field gate at the end of the path

Líthica, the Pedreres de S'Hostal. This photo shows the walls and maze, but there are gardens as well.

CATTLE SHEDS

When a walk takes you through farming country, you will frequently come across small drystone buildings that look like miniature Babylonian ziggurats. These are cattle sheds and are known as *ponts*.

Since Menorca totally lacks building timber, all roofing until recent times was done with stones, hence the need to narrow the span to be covered in this imaginative and unusual way.

It is claimed that some have recently been built to provide homes, not for cattle, but for people, since they do not require planning permission!

Threshing floor near Fornells

THRESHING FLOORS

Just about every farm you pass on your walks will have near it a low, circular, raised stone platform.

These are old threshing floors. Weighted sledges would be dragged round by oxen or donkeys over the cut corn, separating the wheat grains from the chaff as they did so. Throwing the mixture into the wind with broad shovels completes the process.

to the Naveta d'es Tudons (**3h05min**). As you climb the hill on the far side of the valley, notice the circular stone THRESHING FLOORS near the farms on your right (**3h30min**). As you get closer to the city, Ciutadella comes into sight, the cathedral prominent. Raise your eyes and beyond the city you will see the distant fortified farmhouse of Torre del Ram.

One thing to keep your eyes alert for during this long walk are birds. Large birds especially. I have seen more kites, vultures and eagles flying over or perched beside this road than on any other walk on the island. Or anywhere else for that matter.

Eventually the road will bring you back to the CAMÍ VELL DE MAÒ where the walk began (**4h05min**).

Walk 22: CURNIOLA, CALA DE ALGAIARENS AND THE CAVES OF CALA MORELL

See also drawing on page 12
Distance: 13km/8mi; 3h45min
Grade: ● moderate, with ascents/descents of about 150m/500ft overall
Equipment: walking boots (preferably; or comfortable shoes), sunhat, raingear, suncream, picnic, plenty of water, swimwear, towel, binoculars
How to get there and return: 🚗 or 🚌 to/from Cala Morell. Park by the roundabout at the village entrance (40° 3.072'N, 3° 53.079'E).
Alternative walk: Camí de Cavalls (12km/7.4mi; 3h20min; ● grade, access and equipment as main walk). The main walk is a circuit,

but you could do an out-and-back on the Camí de Cavalls from Cala Morell. From the roundabout at the entrance to the village follow Via Lactia 700m northeast to Carrer Auriga (**8**), where you turn right to the 'official' start of the trail (red/white waymarks), just before the coast. Follow it to Cap Gros, retrace steps, then pick up the main walk from the 3h15min-point.
Shorter circuit from Cala de Algaiarens (4km/2.5mi; 1h; ● easy; equipment as above, but trainers will suffice). Park as for Picnic 19, page 17. See notes on page 128.

The his lovely walk makes a very wide circuit round the impressive farmhouse of Curniola, partly through agricultural land and partly through pine woods, and then goes on to explore one of the most important Bronze Age cave settlements in Europe. As a bonus, there are opportunities to enjoy a swim.

FORTIFIED FARMHOUSES
Sometimes you will walk past farmhouses that are attached to large, square, virtually windowless towers. These sturdy dwellings are a feature of the island.

Found also on the mainland in Catalonia, they remind us that Menorca's *calas* attracted quite a different kind of foreign visitor in earlier times — pirates!

The most famous fortified farmhouse on the island is the Torre d'en Quart (left), which you will see during the course of Walk 23.

The fortified farmhouse at Binissaida, shown on page 23, is seen on Walks 4, 6 and 12. Walk 19 passes another good example, Morvedrá Vei.

Left: Torre d'en Quart (Walk 22)

125

THE CAVES AT CALA MORELL

There are many things to look out for, but their sophistication is probably what impresses most. There are paths chipped out of the rock to provide access to them; often windows light them. Usually a central pillar was left to give support to the roof. Frequently niches and troughs have been carved out, and in several there is a raised area where probably the family slept.

As you move up the valley you will come across even more sophisticated features. There is a channel carved out of the cliff face that directs rainwater down to a trough cut out of the cliff, which overflows into an irrigation channel. Another larger channel collects rainwater on the other side of the valley and conveys it to where it was required for irrigation. One cave has an elaborate façade carved in high relief, to give it the appearance of an Egyptian dwelling.

Also of interest are the oval cavities cut into the cliff face.

Similar cavities are found all over the island. Local people called them *'capades de Moro'* (drawing page 12) and attributed them to a Moorish passion for head banging! Their purpose can only be guessed at, and it is assumed that it was funerary, perhaps for holding urns containing bones or ashes, or maybe offerings were placed in them. Near the end of the little valley there is a bridge. Go beyond it to the cave on the right. It has two outstanding features — raised sleeping quarters and a magnificently carved chimney. However, by 1000 BC people had moved out of even these fine caves into the 'up-market' talayotic settlements, and for the next thousand years they were used for burials.

Photo: Cala Morell, from one of the hillside caves

Begin the walk at the **Cala Morell** ROUNDABOUT (**1**): head back TOWARDS CIUTADELLA along the road by which you have come. As you pass the entrance to CURNIOLA (**9min**), you have your first sight of the imposing villa which you will pass again near the end of the walk. A minute later you are opposite another farmhouse — BINI ATRÁM (now a rural hotel), while ahead and to the right you can see one of the most famous farmhouses on the island, the massively defended TORRE D'EN QUART, shown on pages 124-125.

Eventually the main road turns right, past the Torre d'en Quart, towards Ciutadella, and a walled-in, overgrown track goes left to Son Seu farm. Turn left here (**2**; **30min**) for 'Algaiarens' on a narrower little-trafficked road through farmlands, passing the farm of SON ANGEL on the right. Then, leaving the fields behind you, walk through pines and pass

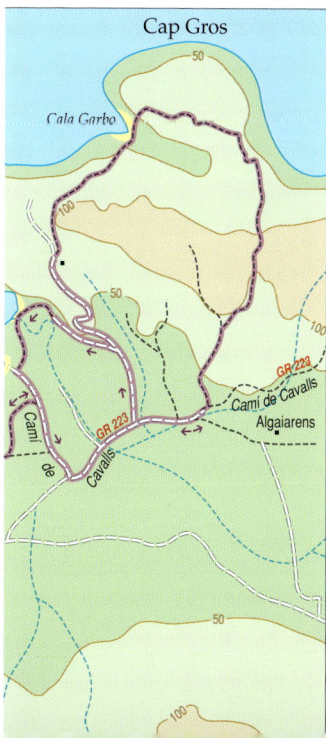
Cap Gros

the gated entrances to the CASETA GUARDA DE SON ANGELS and another house on the left, before turning left and following a track down to the parking area for **Cala de Algaiarens** (**3**; **1h25min**), one of the island's loveliest beaches.

After a swim and a break, walk back the way you came, to the car park and shaded picnic area (Picnic 19). Here you pick up the CAMÍ DE CAVALLS (**4**), heading right, then left, round the car park, with pines to your right. The *Camí* then moves northwest through pines to the fishermen's cove of **Cala Fontanelles** (**5**). Rounding the invigorating cliffs of the **Punta de s'Apres** on a pine-edged path brings you to another track and a signpost at the **Codolar de Biniatramp** (**6**).

Turn right and follow the *Camí* northwest, gently rising in the company of a wall and eventually passing the **Aljub de Corniola** (**7**; **2h15min**), an underground water deposit. The track running parallel with your path, between 100 and 200 metres off to the left, was the earlier route of the *Camí*; beyond it are the fields surrounding the Curniola estate, which you can glimpse from time to time. There are plenty of open shady places to rest, or picnic.

The path brings you back into Cala Morell on CARRER AURIGA (**8**), just south of a turning circle and viewpoint. Follow this road south to a roundabout where you bear left on VIA LACTIA. After about 700m/yds, when you arrive back at the ROUNDABOUT at the entrance to the village (**1**; **3h15min**), keep right, ignoring the road to Ciutadella on your left, still going downhill. It is not long before you see on your left the first pair of CAVES for which Cala

SHORTER CIRCUIT

From the most northerly car park above Cala de Algaiarens follow the signposted Camí de Cavalls east, past a sign pointing left to Platja Tancat, then a second signpost. Just under 500m further on, turn left on another track, *leaving the Camí* and heading towards a gate. Climb the *botador* at the left. Some 200m after turning left, ignore a track on the left and then another one almst at once. But after another 200m, *do* fork left on a cart track and follow it downhill (keeping left some 400m down) to the **Platja d'Es Bot**.

After a swim at this more isolated beach, cross the stream and follow a path to the right of a mini-lagoon. This brings you back to the signpost for Platja Tancat, from where you retrace steps to your car.

But… We think there may be a possibility here for a longer circuit rounding Cap Gros. On the map

we show a path highlighted in violet, taken from various tracings on Google Earth. Unfortunately

Platja d'es Bot (Shorter circuit)

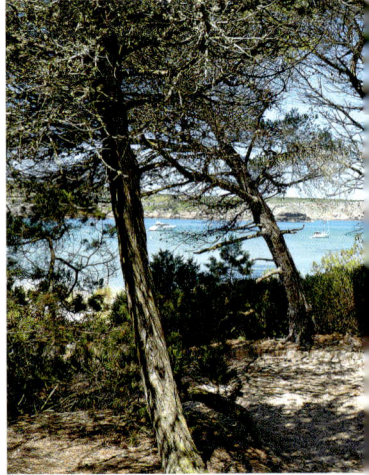

we did not have time on our latest update survey to check its viability. If you would like to try it, be warned: you may encounter path closures at any point!

Morell is famous. After exploring these, carry on down the hill, to where a bridge crosses over the *barranc*. The MAIN TROGLODYTIC VILLAGE (**9**) is situated just before this bridge. Footpaths fork to each side of the hill on your left, and both lead to caves. Most of them are on the left, where they are to be found in the cliffs on both sides of a small valley (Picnic 4).

When you have seen this central part of the village, return to the road and go up the path to the right of the hill. You will soon see two caves some distance away, but as you walk towards them you will discover what seem to be tiny paths cut out from the rock and, when you reach the caves, there is

quite an elaborate road carved to the left of them. These caves connect, and the one on the left is surrounded with little stone troughs.

When you have done with the caves, you may wish to sample Cala Morell's other attraction, its swimming. Return to the road, cross the bridge, and immediately fork right. At the next junction turn right and follow the road down to the beach (a gate part way down prohibits cars). As well as the beach, there is a system of rock paths and sunbathing terraces.

From here steps take you back up to restaurants, bars, and the ROUNDABOUT where you parked (**3h45min**).

Walk 23: ARENAL DE SON SAURA AND THE CAMI DE CAVALLS

Distance: 10.5km/6.5mi; 2h30min

Grade: ● easy; minimal ups and downs

Equipment: comfortable shoes or trainers, sunhat, raingear, suncream, picnic, plenty of water, swimwear, towel, binoculars

How to get there and return: 🚗 to/from Camí de Cavalls signposts on the Me-7, 1km east of the roundabout at its junction with the Me-15 to Fornells (room for a few cars; 40° 1.340'N, 4° 7.263'E). Or 🚌 to/from the roundabout south of Fornells and Ses Salines (add 8-10min walking each way).

Short walk: Me-7 to Arenal de Son Saura (● 5.3km/3.3mi; 1h20min). 🚗 Just walk to the beach, swim and return from Son Parc by bus.

Despite the desirability of circular walks, in many parts of the island the linear *Camí* is the only possibility of access. We were hoping to vary at least *part* of this route, incorporating some sections from the original edition of the book, but all diversions from the *Camí* in this area are firmly off limits these days.

The walk leads to another of the island's spectacular beaches — the Arenal de Son Saura.

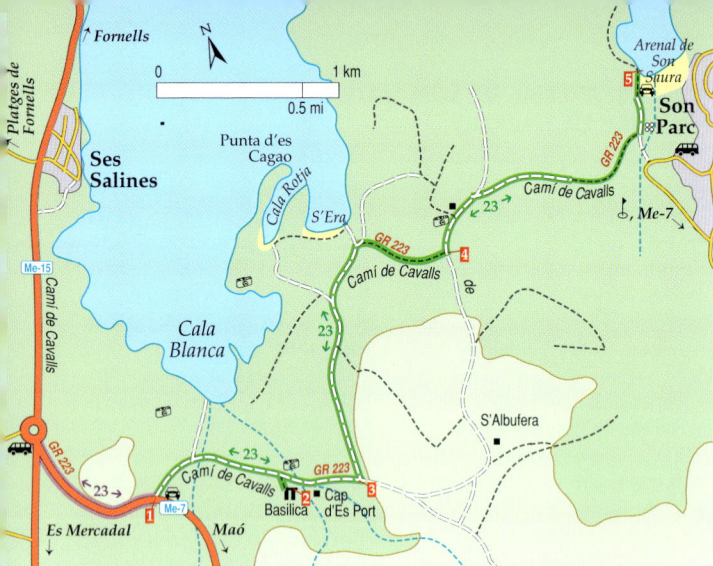

Begin the walk beside the **Me-7** (**1**), just under 1km east of the FORNELLS ROUNDABOUT. Slip between the pillars at the left of the closed gates, to a signpost for the Camí de Cavalls announcing the 'ARENAL DE SON SAURA 4.8 KM'. Follow the wide woodland track, festooned with the blooms of convolvulus and fennel in spring. Straight away you have a good view up to Monte Toro.

After passing a private track to the left, and opposite an *era*, you come to the path up right to the 6th-century **Basílica paleocristiana d'Es Cap des Port** (**2**; **10min**). From the information panel at the top of the modest rise there is a good view over the ruins to the sea.

About 10 minutes later you come to a fork in front of the **Cap d'Es Port** property. This is one of the prettiest spots on the walk: turning left, you cross a gurgling stream on a BRIDGE with fairytale wooden railings. Throughout, the trail is abundantly waymarked with posts in the ground and signposts (see page 31) — so you are unlikely to miss the junction where

the trail goes *sharp left* (**3**; **30min**), leaving the fields for woodland.

After passing a small area where logging may be taking place, you pass two tracks off left. We had been hoping to use them to visit the pretty beach of S'Era, but both are private. Coming to a third track on the left, signs alert you to turn *right* with the *Camí* on a trail rising through more woodland. Meeting another track, turn left (**4**; **55min**) and enjoy some views over the cultivation, marshland and golf course west of Son Parc. After a ruin on the left, you come to a signposted junction where your way is to the right.

Descending, you come down to the left of **Son Parc**'s SEWAGE TREATMENT PLANT and then the car park and the **Arenal de Son Saura**, with a bar/restaurant overlooking the lovely beach (**5**; **1h12min**).

The *Camí* continues from here to Arenal d'en Castell, but those of you who prefer to laze about on the beach can either catch a return bus from outside the Hotel Son Parc or retrace your outgoing route to the **Me-7** (**2h15min**).

Walk 24: FINCA PÚBLICA S'ARANGÍ

Distance: 3.5km/2.2mi; 1h30min
Grade: ● moderate, with some scrambling in rock chaos
Equipment: walking boots or shoes with ankle support, sunhat, raingear, suncream, picnic, water
How to get there and return: 🚗 to/from the Finca pública s'Arangí, almost opposite the KM19 marker on the Me-1 (39° 58.214'N, 4° 5.609'E); or 🚐 bus to/from Es Mercadal, adding 3.5km/2.2mi return
Short walk: Circuits 1 (blue) and 2 (green) (1km/600m; 35min; ● fairly easy, but you must be agile). Follow the main walk to ❸, then head right on the green trail.

The Penya de s'Indi, from the Me-1 viewpoint; do you see the resemblance?

Aside from the Camí de Cavalls, IBANAT (the Balearics' nature conservation organisation) and the island government are creating other walks, for example three bird-watching trails at S'Albufera (Walk 2) and two archaeological trails (PR-IB-Me 1 and PR-IB-Me 2, both of which are shown on the reverse of our touring map). This walk, near the Penya de s'Indi viewpoint, is a small experimental conservation area dedicated to studying the impact of climate change on Menorca's woodlands. There are eight info panels en route — all in Menorquín at present...

Begin the walk at the parking area for **Finca pública s'Arangí** beside the Me-1 (❶). There are a few rustic picnic tables and benches under the trees here, and some signs showing the three routes. For the main walk, take the BLUE TRAIL to the left. It's not a doddle! Watch your footing as the path climbs and descends, twists and turns. When you come to a sign for rock climbers, you're just below the **Penya de s'Indi** (❷) — a rock that looks remarkably like an American Indian's head when viewed from the Me-1.

From here descend to a CONSERVATION AREA (❸; **25min**), with another couple of picnic tables and benches. From here you pick up the RED TRAIL and climb

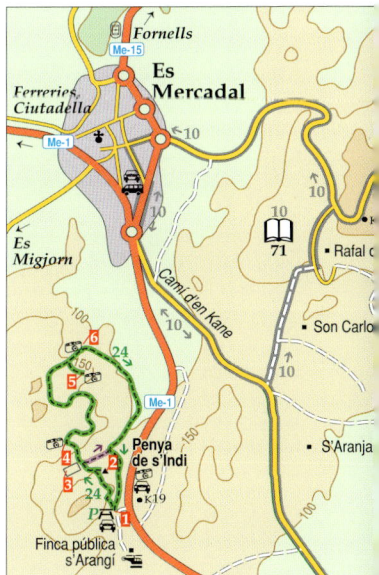

Deep shade in the rock-climbing area below the Penya de s'Indi. Notice the unusual red 'sponge'-like rock in the background.

fairly steeply to the **Mirador de ses Sureres** (**4**), with its fairytale wooden fencing and bench looking up to Monte Toro and down over Alaior. Descend from here past an old SHEEPFOLD, and do another up and down before detouring right to the **Mirador del Toro** (**5**) with view to the eponymous mountain and Es Mercadal. Back on the main trail, a third viewpoint offers much the same views from a stone seating area (**6**; **Mirador des Pi de Tramontana**).

Keep downhill now to find the trail broadening out through lovely woodlands. You meet the green trail — which *is* a doddle, bringing you back to the CAR PARK in 10 minutes (**1h30min**).

BUS TIMETABLES

Most buses are operated by Transportes Menorca SA (TMSA; www.tmsa.es). The main bus stations are in Maó and Ciutadella (see page 7). Other operators are Torres (www.e-torres. net) and Autos Fornells (www.autos fornells. com). *Timetables often change without notice; obtain up-to-date timetables from the web, the bus stations or the tourist office — especially since there are many more bus services than those shown below. These are summer timetables; services may be less frequent from November to April. Journey times are approximate and cumulative.*

SERVICES TO AND FROM MAHON/MAÓ

1 Maó—Alaior—Es Mercadal—Ferreries—Ciutadella *Línia 01, daily, from the bus station in Maó and the Plaça de S'Esplanada in Ciutadella. Journey times: Alaior 15min, Es Mercadal 30min, Ferreries 45min, Ciutadella 1h15min*
Departs Maó (weekdays) 07.15 and hourly until 22.15; (Sat/Sun/holidays) 08.00, 10.00, 11.30, 13.00, 16.00, 18.00, 19.00 21.30
Departs Ciutadella (weekdays) 07.15 and hourly until 22.15; (Sat/Sun/holidays) 08.00, 10.00, 11.30, 13.30, 16.00, 18.00, 20.00, 21.30

1A Maó—Ciutadella express *Línia 14, Mon-Fri only, from the bus station in Maó. Journey time about 50min*
Dep Maó 06.45, 08.00, 08.15, 13.20, 14.20, 15.20, 16.20
Dep Ciutadella 06.45, 08.00, 13.20, 14.20, 15.20, 16.20

2 Maó—Es Castell *Línia 02, daily, from the bus station in Maó. Journey time 10min*
Departs Maó 07.20*, 07.45*, 08.15*, 08.45*; half-hourly from 09.15 to 10.45; from 11.45 to 13.45, 14.15*, 14.45*, 15.15*; from 15.45 to 16.45; from 17.45 to 20.45
Departs Es Castell 07.30*, 08.00*, 08.30*, 09.00*; then half-hourly from 09.30 to 11.00; from 12.00 to 14.00; 14.30*, 15.00*, 15.30*; and from 16.00 to 21.00

3 Maó—Sant Lluís *Línia 03, daily, from the bus station in Maó. Journey time 10min*
Departs Maó 07.15*, 08.10*, 08.30*; then hourly from 09.30 to 13.30; 15.15; hourly from 16.30 to 19.30; then 20.15
Departs Sant Lluís 07.30*, 08.20; then hourly from 09.50 to 12.50; 15.45; then hourly from 16.50 to 19.50

4 Maó—Punta Prima *Línia 92, daily, from Maó bus station. Journey time 25min*
Departs Maó 07.00*, 08.00*; hourly from 09.00 to 13.00; 14.00*, 15.00*; hourly from 16.00-19.00; and finally at 20.00*, 21.00*, 22.00*, 23.00*; returns from Punta Prima (in front of Hotel Xaloc) 30 minutes later

5 Maó—Alcaufar—S'Algar—Las Palmeras *Línia 91, daily, from Maó bus station. Journey times: Alcaufar 15min, Las Palmeras 25min, S'Algar 30min*
Departs Maó 08.30, 09.30, 12.30, 13.30, 15.30, 18.30; returns from S'Algar 30 minutes later

6 Maó—Binibèquer *Línia 93, daily, from Maó bus station. Journey time 25min*
Departs Maó 10.30, 14.20, 17.30; returns from Binibèquer 11.00, 14.35, 18.00

7 Maó—Sant Climent—Son Vitamina—Cala'n Porter *Línia 31, Mon-Sat from Maó bus station. Journey times: Sant Climent 10min, Son Vitamina 15min, Cala'n Porter 20min*
Departs Maó 09.30, 10.30, 11.45, 13.30, 16.00, 18.00, 19.40
Departs Cala'n Porter 10.00, 11.00, 12.15, 13.45, 16.30, 18.30, 20.00

8 Maó—Es Grau *daily (July-Sept only), from Maó bus station. Journey time 25min*
Departs Maó 10.00, 11.00■, 12.00*, 13.00■, 17.00
Departs Es Grau 10.30, 11.30■, 12.30*, 13.30■, 17.30

9 Maó—Alaior—Torre Solí-Nou—Club San Jaime—Son Bou *Línia 32, Mon-Sat, from Maó bus station. Journey times: Alaior 10min, Torre Solí-Nou 25min, Club San Jaime/Son Bou 30min*
Departs Maó 08.30, 10.00, 11.30, 13.00, 17.00, 18.30, 20.00; returns from Son Bou one hour later

*except Sun/holidays; ■ only Sun/holidays

134   Landscapes of Menorca

10 Maó—Sant Tomàs *Linea 71, daily, from Maó bus station. Journey time 45min*
Departs Maó 08.00*, 08.15■, 10.15*, 11.15■, 12.30*, 14.15■, 15.15*, 17.30*, 18.30■, 19.45*; returns 50min later (Mon-Sat), 35min later (Sun/holidays)

11 Maó—Arenal d'en Castell—Son Parc—Fornells *daily, from J A Clavé 7 (private bus company, not TMSA). Journey times: Arenal 30min, Son Parc 55min, Fornells 1h10min*
Dep Maó 11.00, 13.00*, 19.00; Departs Fornells 08.30■, 09.00*, 15.45*, 17.00■
Dep Son Parc 15min later and Arenal 40min later

12 Maó—Cala Santa Galdana *Linea 51, daily, from Maó bus station. Journey time 45 minutes*
Departs Maó 09.30*, 10.30■, 16.15*, 17.30■; returns about 50 minutes later

SERVICES TO AND FROM CIUTADELLA: see also (1 and 1A) above

13 Ciutadella—Sant Tomàs *Linea 72, daily from TMSA, Plaça dels Pins. Journey 1h*
Departs Ciutadella 08.00*, 10.15*, 11.40■, 12.30*, 14.40■, 15.15*, 17.30*, 18.30■, 19.45*
Departs Sant Tomàs 08.35*, 10.50*, 12.15■, 13.20*, 15.15■, 15.50*, 18.05*, 19.05■, 20.35*

14 Ciutadella—Santandría—Cala Blanca *daily** from Plaça de S'Esplanada. Journey times: Santandría 10min, Cala Blanca 15min*
Departs Ciutadella 07.00, 08.00, 09.00, 09.40*, 10.10, 10.40*, 11.15, 11.50, 12.30*, 13.15, 13.45*, 14.15*, 14.45*, 15.15*, 16.00, 17.00*, 18.00, 19.00, 20.00*, 21.00, 22.20; returns from Cala Blanca about 25 minutes later

15 Ciutadella—Cala'n Bosch—Son Xoriguer *daily** from Plaça de S'Esplanada. Journey times: Cala'n Bosch 15min, Son Xoriguer 20min*
Departs Ciutadella 07.00, 08.00, and from 08.45* to 14.30 every 15min

*except Sun/holidays; ■ only Sun/holidays
**service of the Torres bus company, with departures from the Plaça de S'Esplanada

(every 30min on Sundays); then 15.00 to 23.30 every 30min (every hour on the half hour on Sundays); return times about 20 minutes later
Also **Cala Blanes—Cala'n Bosch** *daily:* Departs 09.10, 11.00; returns 12.45, 17.20
Also **Son Blanc—Cala'n Bosch** *daily:* Departs 10.15; returns 15.45
Also **Cala Blanca—Cala'n Bosch** *daily:* Departs 10.25; returns 15.45

16 Ciutadella—Cala Santa Galdana *Linea 52, daily, from TMSA, Plaça dels Pins. Journey time about 30min.*
Departs Ciutadella 09.50■, 10.40*, 13.50, 16.45
Departs Cala Santa Galdana 10.00*, 10.20■, 13.20, 16.20*, 17.20■
Also **Ciutadella—Ferreries—Cala Santa Galdana** *Linea 53; see Timetable 19 below*

17 Ciutadella—Los Delfines—Cala Forcat *daily** from Plaça de S'Esplanada*
Departs Ciutadella 07.15*, 08.15*, 08.40, 09.05, 09.35*, 09.50, 10.05*, 10.30, 10.50*, 11.05, 11.30*, 11.55, 12.30*, 13.00, 13.30*, 14.00, 14.30*, 15.00*, 15.30, 16.00*, 16.30, 17.00*, 17.30, 18.00*, 18.30, 19.15, 20.00, 20.45; returns 10 minutes later

18 Ciutadella—Son Blanc—Sa Caleta *daily** from Plaça de S'Esplanada*
Departs Ciutadella 08.50, 10.10, 11.10*, 12.05, 13.00, 14.05*, 15.00*, 16.20, 17.30*, 18.30, 19.30, 20.30*; returns 5 minutes later

19 Ciutadella—Cala Morell *daily** from Plaça de S'Esplanada*
Departs Ciutadella 11.20, 15.15, 18.30; returns about 15 minutes later

SERVICES TO AND FROM FERRERIES (run by TMSA): see also (1) and (16) above

20 Ferreries—Cala Santa Galdana *Linea 53, daily. Journey time 15min. These connect with the Maó—Ciutadella—Maó service (1).*
Departs Ciutadella 07.05*, 08.05*, 09.05, 09.40*, 10.05-13.05 hourly, 15.05*, 16.05, 16.50*, 17.05-20.05 hourly, 21.05*, 22.05*; returns 15 minutes later

Index

Geographical names comprise the only entries in this index; for other entries, see Contents, page 3. A page number in **bold type** indicates a photograph or drawing, a page number in *italics* a map; both may be in addition to a text reference on the same page. (*TM* refers to the large-scale walking map on the reverse of the fold-out touring map).

135